What Others Are Saying About *Leadership Awakening:*
Foundational Principles for Lasting Success...

"Doug strives to follow God in good times and in bad, and to challenge others to do the same. We are in desperate need of a leadership and spiritual awakening in our nation. Building upon lasting foundational principles, Doug is working tirelessly to plant the seeds for that awakening and revival."

—*Bobby Jindal*
Former Governor of Louisiana

"True leadership is a calling, not a convenience. In the midst of great personal crises, Doug displayed his calling with the 'peace that surpasses understanding.' Some talk, others lead. Doug is among the latter."

—*Greg Abbott*
Governor of Texas

"My friend Doug Stringer has written a courageous book out of the principles he personally exemplifies. His life speaks through this book. Though he says it well, well done is still better than well said. This book lays the foundation for how to finish well in life."

—*Bishop Dale Carnegie Bronner*
Founder and senior pastor, Word of Faith Cathedral, Atlanta, GA

"Doug Stringer has accomplished amazing things, and his organization, Somebody Cares, is one of the best in the nation. He models the leadership teachings of Jesus, and as a result, is one of the most effective leaders in the country. He has taken that leadership experience and put it in this excellent book, *Leadership Awakening.* Now you have an opportunity to learn some of the simple yet profound lessons that have made Doug so unique, and that will make you, too, into a leader."

—*David Barton*
Best-selling author
Founder, WallBuilders

"In *Leadership Awakening,* my friend Doug Stringer offers a lifetime of wisdom and biblical insight on how to not only overcome the obstacles all leaders will inevitably face, but also how to become the battle-hardened leader whom God can use to fulfill His plans for the forthcoming great spiritual awakening."

—*Troy Anderson*
Pulitzer Prize-nominated journalist
Author, *The Babylon Code*

"Doug Stringer is a true hero, acknowledged as a champion advocate and mobilizer of ministry by many city churches since the founding and advancing of Somebody Cares Houston! Doug is among the five most effective parachurch leaders I have known in my fifty years of service."

—*Jack W. Hayford*
Founder and Chancellor, The King's University, Southlake, Texas
Pastor Emeritus, The Church on the Way, Van Nuys, California

"Doug Stringer's life embodies both leadership and endurance. His commitment to Christ, his integrity, and his passion for serving others have been a transformative demonstration of leadership—one worthy of emulating. Accordingly, our dark times require prophetic leadership, people who are committed to issuing a clarion call to followers of Jesus to be holy, to be one, and to be the light. Doug's teachings and, more important, his life raise the volume on that call, all the while reconciling truth with love."

—*Rev. Samuel Rodriguez*
President, National Hispanic Christian Leadership Conference and
Hispanic Evangelical Association

"Prayer warrior, leader, man of God—Doug Stringer issues a compelling call to each of us to be a leader that lasts. This is a unique moment in history—now is the time for leaders to rise up and lead."

—*Dr. Ronnie Floyd*
Former president, Southern Baptist Convention
Senior Pastor, Cross Church, Springdale, Arkansas

"*Leadership Awakening* inspires us to rise and shine in the midst of great challenges and uncertainty, and to dream God-sized dreams. His prayer-driven leadership awakened a spirit of reconciliation among many people, in South Carolina and beyond, to help prepare our state to demonstrate grace and love to the world in the wake of difficult times. Doug reminds us that, now more than ever, Jesus is calling leaders to awaken to His great power and purpose."

—*Rev. Jeff Kersey*
Lead pastor, Mt. Horeb United Methodist Church, Lexington, SC

"Doug Stringer reminds us of the basics of real leadership—the lessons we must learn are not easy but well worth the effort. All too often, we want to soar, but we have not laid a strong foundation. The book admirably provides the way and the motivation to live like strong leaders."

—*Ken Eldred*
Author, *The Integrated Life*
Cofounder and CEO, Living Stones Foundation

"In *Leadership Awakening*, Doug Stringer discusses the genuine spiritual disciplines through which the Holy Spirit develops successful leaders in the midst of 'cosmetic' Christianity. Doug shares how God adjusted him through the Word, and how God can develop a credible champion dedicated to the care of others."

—*Tom Phillips*
Vice President, Billy Graham Evangelistic Association
Executive Director, Billy Graham Library, Charlotte, North Carolina

"As I reflected on the multiple insights in this book, I could not help but think that Doug Stringer's ministry, Somebody Cares, emphasizes first and foremost that God cares. This book describes the power of one person, surrendered to God, who started a movement teaching that *anyone* can learn to care. Leadership is a process, and Doug Stringer's lessons are lifesaving ropes for climbers on the mountain of the Christian life."

—*Doug Beacham*
Presiding Bishop, International Pentecostal Holiness Church,
Oklahoma City, Oklahoma

"Doug Stringer provides a compelling and comprehensive examination of the foundational principles of a Christ-centered *Leadership Awakening*—a must-read for those who aim to run their respective races with divine strength and confidence, and, most importantly, for those who aim to 'finish well.'"

—*Dr. Karen Kossie-Chernyshev*
Professor of History, Texas Southern University
Minister of Music, Latter Day Deliverance Revival Church, Houston, Texas

"I have watched the ongoing work of the Holy Spirit in Doug Stringer's life, making him an outstanding leader in our day. God has raised up Doug to spiritually awaken men and women leaders to the desperate needs of our culture and to minister to those needs. *Leadership Awakening* is a must-read for those who desire to impact 'the day' for God's glory!"

—*Dr. Steve Riggle*
Founding Pastor, Grace Community Church, Houston, Texas
President, Grace International Churches

"Doug Stringer's life exemplifies the humility of submission to the Lord, first and foremost. Being led by the Lord, we will develop and sustain authentic, servant leadership, bearing much fruit for the kingdom of God."

—*Lisa Crump*
COO, National Day of Prayer Task Force

"Doug Stringer has challenged my leadership. He has stretched my thinking to embrace others and see my calling as larger than my assignment as a local church leader. I am a better leader because of Doug's ministry and message."

—*Garrett Booth*
Senior Pastor, Grace Community Church, Houston, Texas

"I love it! Short paragraphs...short chapters...compelling illustrations and quotes... personal stories...confirming Scripture! More than leadership lessons, *Leadership Awakening* offers life lessons, as well. My sons will receive copies of this book! It is a fathomless resource of insight and inspiration from a father in the faith, and it captures the profound and the practical."

—*Dr. Jeff Farmer*
President, Pentecostal/Charismatic Churches of North America
Former President, Open Bible Churches

"Leadership is proven, not just preached. Doug's track record of remarkable success and reach will be your road map to significance in kingdom ministry."

—*Dr. Roger Parrott*
President, Belhaven University

"Doug Stringer clearly expresses that leadership, in all its facets, is more about the life, character, and constant spiritual formation of the leader than about successful results. It is my privilege to recommend this insightful manual to those of us who are called and charged to lead."

—*Dr. Randall J. Pannell*
Interim President and Vice President of Academics, North Greenville University

"Doug Stringer's compassionate outreaches to thousands, along with his networking skills, integrity, and patience under trial, have given him vast influence among several generations."

—*Bishop Joseph Mattera*
Founder, Christ Covenant Coalition

"This book will stretch you to always excel in pleasing the Lord, whether you are a young or old, new or seasoned minister of the gospel. Doug Stringer shares many nuggets of wisdom he gained not as theories but as genuine experiences through the years."

—*Dr. Paul Tan*
Apostolic Overseer, City Blessing Churches
President, World Blessing Foundation and Indonesian Relief Fund

"If anyone understands the intricacies of leadership, Doug Stringer does. God has given him insight into the challenges, struggles, and discouragements. If ever we needed a leadership awakening, we need it today.."

—*Bishop Angel L. Núñez*
Senior Pastor, Bilingual Christian Church
President, Multicultural Prayer Movement

"Dr. Stringer is able to succinctly describe, with biblical examples and real life stories, the calling and challenges of being a Christian leader. His ability to identify the attributes of great leaders is inspiring, and a must-read for anyone wanting to understand what it takes to overcome the temptations and pitfalls of Christian leadership."

—*Jay E. Mincks*
Executive Vice President, Insperity Inc.

"Doug Stringer is one of the most authentic ministers and credible leaders I have the great honor of knowing. This book is an invaluable deposit of Doug's heartfelt passion and real-life pain, as well as his staunch perseverance in the process of true servant ministry. The wisdom purchased in this book graciously points current and future leaders to the root structures of lasting transformational leadership."

—*Jayde Duncan*
Senior Pastor, Antioch Church, Colorado Springs, Colorado

"Doug Stringer appeals to us to move beyond superficiality, 'cosmetic Christianity,' and even the judgmental spirit of Pharisees. Instead, he urges us to embody the biblical truths we hold dear, with authenticity, fervency, and consistency. He challenges us to seek to love, serve, and restore, and to be willing to make a difference at great sacrifice. Doug has not only picked out leadership principles and explained them clearly, he has also formulated concise leadership strategies and patterns that could be taught and applied anywhere—especially in the marketplace."

—*Tan Sri (Dr.) Francis Yeoh*
YTL Corporation & YTL Group

"Just when I wondered if anything new could be written on leadership, Doug Stringer stepped forward. Think of *Leadership Awakening* as twenty-five power-packed vignettes, each rich in practical counsel, each worthy of deep reflection. This book is designed to help you finish strong. It masterfully achieves that goal."

—*John D. Beckett*
Chairman, The Beckett Companies
Author, *Loving Monday* and *Mastering Monday*

Acknowledgments

Relationships define our destinies. Over the years I've come to recognize this truth. Whatever influence or successes I've had in my life are due to relationships—first with God, then with others. I am grateful to all those who have invested, influenced, encouraged, and journeyed with me throughout the years.

I would also like to thank those who believed in the message of this book and worked hard to see that it was brought to completion. A special thanks to Jim Buchan for all his research and editing expertise, and to Belinda, Alison, Susie, Jodie, and others for all the time proof reading, reading, and re-reading to make sure the content and message was communicated with my heart and intent.

A very special thank you to Bob Whitaker Jr., Christine Whitaker, and all the wonderful people at Whitaker House for nudging me to get this important and timely message out. Thank you for your investment, trust, and encouragement. Thank you to Tom Cox at Whitaker House for the value of your time and patience working through all the details and final layout of the book.

Finally, I want to say how grateful I am for my wife, Lisa, for being a sounding board and for working with me many a late night going over and over the manuscript throughout the entire process.

LEADERSHIP
AWAKENING

DOUG
STRINGER

WHITAKER
HOUSE

LEADERSHIP AWAKENING:
Foundational Principles for Lasting Success

www.dougstringer.com
www.somebodycares.org

ISBN: 978-1-62911-736-2
eBook ISBN: 978-1-62911-737-9
Printed in the United States of America
© 2016 by Doug Stringer

Whitaker House
1030 Hunt Valley Circle
New Kensington, PA 15068
www.whitakerhouse.com

Library of Congress Cataloging-in-Publication Data
Names: Stringer, Doug, author.
Title: Leadership awakening : foundational principles for lasting success / by Doug Stringer.
Description: New Kensington, PA : Whitaker House, 2016. | Includes bibliographical references.
Identifiers: LCCN 2016032999 (print) | LCCN 2016033477 (ebook) | ISBN 9781629117362 (trade pbk. : alk. paper) | ISBN 9781629117379 (E-book)
Subjects: LCSH: Christian leadership. | Success--Religious aspects--Christianity.
Classification: LCC BV652.1 .S775 2016 (print) | LCC BV652.1 (ebook) | DDC 253--dc23
LC record available at https://lccn.loc.gov/2016032999

2 3 4 5 6 7 8 9 10 11 12 **U** 24 23 22 21 20 19 18 17

Contents

Preface: Finishing the Race Well

Tanzanian John Stephen Akhwari was considered one of the best marathon runners in the world. He participated in the 1968 Olympics in Mexico City but wasn't accustomed to the high altitude. At about the halfway mark, he collided with another runner. Akhwari was injured, hurting both his knee and shoulder; yet he continued the race with bandages and considerable pain—limping, walking, and jogging to the finish.

Of the seventy-five who started the race, only fifty-seven finished. Akhwari was number fifty-seven—dead last. When he crossed the finish line, people asked him, "Why did you continue the race when you were injured and in such pain?"

He replied, "My nation did not send me thousands of kilometers to start a race, but rather to finish the race."

God didn't just call you to *start* the race; He called you to finish the race—and He wants you to *finish well*. Yet too often, this isn't the case with men and women God calls to lead His people. In fact, Dr. J. Robert Clinton of Fuller Theological Seminary has been quoted as saying that an estimated 70 percent of all leaders, biblically and historically, do *not* finish the race well.

There is an erosion and unraveling of so many of our moral foundations. We need a *Leadership Awakening*! We need a *Leadership Awakening* for the vacuum of godly and courageous leaders that exists today. Education alone doesn't make or produce them, Diplomas don't prove them. Character does! Degrees on leadership are only worth the paper they're written on, without the substance of character to go with it.

I've written this book to illuminate the forces that war against Christian leaders, as well as the powerful resources God has given them to live in victory. Let me be clear: This is not a book based on untested theories or the latest fads about Christian leadership. Rather, it's filled with truths I've gleaned over thirty years of personal experience and biblical application, both in business and in ministry. To that end, throughout this book I am also including quotations of mine that I call "Provoke-a-Thoughts." These are sayings I have used throughout my work and ministry that seem to have resonated in the lives of others over the years. I hope they provoke your own thoughts about what it takes to become a leader who lasts.

I've discovered that when you build your life on the proper foundations, you don't have to fear how your story will end. Like King David, you will be able to confidently declare, "*Surely goodness and mercy shall follow me all the days of my life; and I will dwell in the house of the Lord forever*" (Psalm 23:6).

That is my prayer for you as I write these pages. May your life be marked by God's goodness and mercy all the way until you reach your finish line on earth, leaving a lasting legacy for those who follow.

—Doug Stringer

1

Why So Many
Tragic Endings?

If Dr. J. Robert Clinton is correct that such a large percentage of Christian leaders don't finish the race well, then it's crucial to learn lessons from those who have succeeded in avoiding the enemy's traps. Clinton has identified six key areas in which many leaders stumble:

1. Finances

2. Power

3. Pride

4. Sexual temptation

5. Family issues

6. Loss of spiritual momentum

I'm convinced that discouragement underlies many of these specific pitfalls; it is one of satan's favorite weapons to use against leaders. Christian leaders are called to lead God's people to a place of promise and destiny, but it's impossible for them to do that if they are disillusioned, disappointed, or distracted along the way.

Effective leaders are able to maintain their vision, hold on to their hope, and continually fan into flame their passion for God and their compassion for hurting people. But it's not enough to do these things *sporadically*—they must do them *consistently* and *intentionally*.

Back to the Basics

I have rarely seen a leader fall because of failing to grasp some deep theological treatise. The reason leaders stumble along the way is not because they don't understand Hebrew or Greek. Nor do they get off track because they misinterpret the book of Revelation or some other prophetic passages in God's Word. In many cases, leaders get into trouble because they neglect fundamental truths and basic spiritual disciplines. Let me explain with an illustration from one of the most successful football coaches of all time.

At age forty-five, Vince Lombardi became a head football coach in the NFL for the first time in his life. It was 1959, and he had the challenging task of leading the Green Bay Packers, a team that had won only two games the previous season. He clearly had his work cut out for him. But Lombardi wasn't going to let last year's record shape his expectations. After all, this was a *new season.*

When the discouraged NFL players gathered for their first preseason meeting, they must have wondered how their new coach was planning to turn things around. Coach Lombardi entered the locker room and stood silently for several seconds. Holding out a football in front of these men, he spoke one of the most famous lines in football history: "Gentlemen, this is a football."

In just five words, the new coach had communicated his philosophy for the team's success: They were going to start with the basics and make sure to execute the fundamentals. You see, the Packers had been losing not because they lacked talent but because they'd forgotten the basics of football.

This simple story is a powerful message for us as leaders. We can read countless leadership books and attend all the latest seminars on how to build a successful organization. But in the final analysis, our success or failure as leaders will be determined by how well we executed the basics of the Christian life.

Vince Lombardi brought the Packers a new philosophy that led to incredible success in the following years, including several league championships and Super Bowl victories. A seemingly hopeless team was given a new beginning.

What a great lesson! No matter how poorly things may have gone for you in the past, God can turn things around amazingly fast. However, the key to your turnaround is the same key that led the Packers to victory—you have to get back to the *basics*.

Beyond the Superficial

When I say the basics, I don't mean a superficial or shallow spiritual life. Too many Christians—even those in leadership—have spiritual lifestyles akin to the old commercials for Brylcreem, the hair-styling gel: "A little dab'll do ya!" This is certainly not the philosophy we want to have when it comes to spiritual disciplines like prayer, fasting, and Bible study.

We can't expect to have powerful ministries if we have a "Now I lay me down to sleep" prayer life. I'll never forget the day Leonard Ravenhill told me, "Brother Doug, God doesn't answer prayer; He answers desperate prayer." Rather than settling for token, superficial prayers, Christian leaders must learn to wrestle with God and passionately pursue His blessing on their lives. (See Genesis 32:24–32.)

In the same way, we'll never consistently live in victory just by memorizing a few favorite Bible verses to quote. We should consistently take time to saturate ourselves with God's presence and His Word. His Word must be written on our hearts, and we must be committed to applying it in every area of our life. (See Psalm 40:6–8; Ezra 7:10.)

As Bible teacher J. Vernon McGee used to say, it's not enough to carry a big leather Bible if we haven't ingested its teachings and put them into practice. He said we must "put the Word of God into shoe leather," walking it out in every aspect of our life. That's the only way to consistently stand in victory and turn the world upside down for Christ.

The first-century Christians showed how powerful the basics can be. They were known as *"uneducated and untrained men,"* yet they rocked the world! How did this happen? Because *"they had been with Jesus"* (Acts 4:13).

The day of Pentecost had brought these early disciples a new beginning. In a moment's time, they received power from on high—reversing all the failure and frustration that had gone on before. Instead of denying, doubting, or betraying their Lord, now they were bold witnesses. (See Acts 1:8; 2:1–4.) No matter how discouraged you may be at the moment, *you* can experience this same kind of turnaround!

Maintaining Your Passion

Just like us, the early Christians were tempted to get busy with other things and lose sight of the basics that had given them such strength and favor. But God brought them back to a renewed commitment, and they resolved, "*We will give ourselves continually to prayer and to the ministry of the word*" (Acts 6:4). Furthermore, going back to the basics resulted in a time of breakthrough for the church in Jerusalem: "*Then the word of God spread, and the number of the disciples multiplied greatly*" (Acts 6:7). It will do the same for us today.

Sadly, though, we later read in Revelation that some of the churches that began with great power and authority were in danger of not finishing well. The believers in Ephesus were full of admirable works, but they had lost their "*first love*" (Revelation 2:4) for the Lord. Jesus said the church in Sardis was spiritually "*dead*" (Revelation 3:1). And the Christians in Laodicea were so lukewarm that Jesus said He was going to spit them out of His mouth. (See Revelation 3:15–16.)

> **PROVOKE-A-THOUGHT:**
>
> "WE CANNOT CHANGE OUR PAST, BUT THE CHOICES WE MAKE EACH DAY DETERMINE OUR FUTURE."

What a sobering message for us as kingdom leaders. Just as Paul wrote to his spiritual son Timothy, God would say to us today, "*Stir up the gift of God which is in you*" (2 Timothy 1:6). In other translations, Paul compares us to waning embers of fire that must be continually fanned into flame, or rekindled.

You see, the world won't be changed by dead religion or empty theology, but by Christians whose hearts are aflame with passion for God. We will once again turn the world upside down when we return to our first Love and consistently practice the basics of our faith.

In words that now sound prophetic, Salvation Army founder William Booth warned,

> I consider that the chief dangers which confront the coming century will be religion without the Holy Ghost, Christianity without Christ, forgiveness without repentance, salvation without regeneration, politics without God, and heaven without hell.

Today the church is blessed with many gifted orators and well-trained communicators, but we need much more than that. In order for the church to be transformed, we must have leaders who spend time in the presence of God. We need men and women who hear from Him and communicate His heart to a desperate world. And this means they must love the Lord and His people more than they love their career, ministry, or even their own lives.

It's Not over Till It's Over

In the chapters that follow, I'll be sharing some vital principles on how you can not only experience success in your leadership role but experience *lasting* success. You see, it is very important how the game of life ends. If you're on a basketball or football team, you know that it's nice when your team has the lead in the first three quarters of the game, but it's tragic if your team blows the lead in the fourth quarter.

In this paraphrase from *The Message*, the apostle Paul gives a colorful description of what it takes to finish well and be a gold medalist in God's kingdom:

> *You've all been to the stadium and seen the athletes race. Everyone runs; one wins. Run to win. All good athletes train hard. They do it for a gold medal that tarnishes and fades. You're after one that's gold eternally. I don't know about you, but I'm running hard for the finish line. I'm giving it everything I've got. No sloppy living for me! I'm staying alert and in top condition. I'm not going to get caught napping, telling*

everyone else all about it and then missing out myself.

(1 Corinthians 9:24–27 MSG)

Paul warns that a runner needs to run hard and stay alert in order successfully reach the finish line. He says he wants to make sure he doesn't miss out on God's best.

Some of you reading this book may wonder if it's too late to finish well. Perhaps you've fallen into some kind of sin and you doubt your life can ever be the same again. Or maybe you've hit a wall on your marathon through life. Perhaps your chosen career or ministry seems too difficult, and you feel like giving up.

Let me encourage you with the words of the great American philosopher and baseball Hall of Famer Yogi Berra: "It ain't over till it's over." Isn't that good news? As long as there's still breath in your lungs, the game isn't over. There's still hope for a turnaround. The gold medal can still be yours.

PROVOKE-A-THOUGHT:

OUR TRUE LEGACY COMES NOT FROM THE SERMONS WE PREACH OR HOW MANY PEOPLE FOLLOW US ON TWITTER OR OTHER SOCIAL MEDIA. IT'S NOT THE SIZE OF OUR CHURCH OR MINISTRY. THE LIVES WE LIVE BEFORE WE ENTER THE PORTALS OF ETERNITY WILL DETERMINE THE INFLUENCE WE HAVE AND THE INFLUENCE WE WILL LEAVE FOR THE NEXT GENERATION.

Dr. Edwin Louis Cole, founder of the Christian Men's Network, said it this way: "Champions are not those who never fail, but those who never quit." He used to point out that Jesus refused to quit and pressed on to fulfill His mission even though it cost Him everything. Despite the agony of the Cross, our Lord was resurrected, and He's able to bring resurrection to *your* hopes and dreams, too. Even if you've grievously departed from your high calling in Christ, the Bible says that you can *"rise again"* (Proverbs 24:16). You can bounce back from failure and frustration, having even more influence than you've ever had before.

Hebrews 12:1 says the grandstand is full of heroes of the faith who are cheering you on to victory. Through faith, they finished their races well, and now it's your turn. The example you set and the legacy you leave can set the pace for a whole new generation of champions, impacting the world for Jesus.

2

Aligned with God's Kingdom Purposes

When my body gets out of whack, sometimes I have to go to my chiropractor for an adjustment. Often, he makes small adjustments to my spine, yet it makes a big difference in how I feel. In the same way, proper alignments play a critical role in our success or failure as Christian leaders. Misalignments, on the other hand, can cripple leaders and prevent them from fulfilling their calling and finishing well.

Over the years, I've concluded that a leader's influence and authority are basically derived from proper alignments, agreements, associations, and attitudes. Sometimes I even write them out as if they were a mathematical equation:

Proper Alignments

+ Proper Agreements

+ Proper Associations

+ Proper Attitudes

= Kingdom Authority

If any one of these ingredients is missing from the equation, a leader's influence will be diminished or will disappear entirely. This is not always clear, because none of these factors are static and unchanging. We have all seen men and women of God who squander their kingdom authority and spiritual anointing by making choices that take them out of proper alignment.

Fortunately, God can restore us and correct our misalignments. When our lives get out of balance, He can help us get things back in order. But once again, this requires intentionality on our part. We have to get back to the basics, restoring our prayer life, worship, and devotion to God's Word. And if our stewardship is out of alignment, we must take steps of faith and be generous with the time, talents, and resources the Lord has given us.

I don't know if the roads in your city have many potholes or speed bumps, but driving over them can really mess up your vehicle's alignment; you might even have to get it realigned at the repair shop. Likewise, life is full of bumpy roads, and sometimes they can cause us discouragement, disappointment, and even disillusionment.

PROVOKE-A-THOUGHT:

"OFTENTIMES WE CREATE OUR WORLD BY HOW WE CHOOSE TO PRIORITIZE WHAT IS MOST IMPORTANT TO US."

Sometimes it's very confusing when our lives gets out of whack. It's not always easy to tell what causes it, either—whether we've strayed from the Lord in some way, whether it's an attack from the enemy, or whether we are just experiencing the normal stresses of life.

During confusing times like that, I use a little litmus test to sort things out. I ask myself whether I've been allowing harmful things to enter into my spirit or mind through my eyes or ears. If I've allowed improper things into my life, I should not be surprised when I end up experiencing negative thoughts or weird dreams.

That's why I've found it so vitally important to set my mind on the Lord right before I go to sleep, so that He is my last thought at night and my first thought when I get up. If that has not been your practice, I encourage you to give it a try. I'm convinced that if you intentionally make the

Lord the Alpha (at the beginning of your day) and Omega (at the close of your day), the *rest* of your day will be transformed as well.

"High Noon" in God's Sunlight

An interesting biblical example of spiritual alignment is found in James 1:17: *"Every good gift and every perfect gift is from above, and comes down from the Father of lights, with whom there is no variation or shadow of turning."*

James' reference to God *"with whom there is no shadow of turning"* refers to sundials, a common device for telling time back in his day. They didn't have clocks or watches, so sundials were their best option. At exactly high noon, there was no shadow on the sundial. Why? Because the earth was perfectly aligned with the sun.

How does this apply to you and me? When we're at high noon, or in proper alignment, there is no shadow around us. Just as a sundial must be aligned with the *sun* to cast no shadow, our lives as Christian leaders must be aligned with God's *Son* to cast no shadow.

Furthermore, the sun doesn't revolve around the earth, as many people believed centuries ago. Instead, the earth revolves around the sun. Spiritually speaking, the same is true: We must come to the clear understanding that God doesn't revolve us, but we revolve around Him.

If you're waiting for God to change, you're going to get very frustrated. In quite unmistakable terms, He has declared, *"I am the Lord, I do not change"* (Malachi 3:6). And in the same way, Scripture tells us, *"Jesus Christ is the same yesterday, today, and forever"* (Hebrews 13:8).

So if neither God the Father nor God the Son is going to change, who must do the changing? You and me! God will never allow Himself to be conformed to *our* image or expectations, but He wants to transform us into *His* image and bring us into alignment with *His* plans.

But let's be honest, as crazy as it sounds, we have all had times when we thought we knew better than God. We've done things *our* way instead of *His* way, and we've reaped negative consequences. We could avoid so many problems if we would just keep in mind Winkie Pratney's great maxim, "He is God, and I am not." When we align our lives with His purposes, we have authority in His name to rebuke the devil and our negative circumstances.

But when we allow ourselves to drift away from our "high noon" position, we'll see shadows begin to appear around us; and if we don't take corrective action, the faint shadows will eventually turn to darkness. Remember, when shadows or darkness appear in our spiritual lives, it's not because *God* moved. He remains constant, and it's necessary for us to re-align ourselves with His character and His will. Often, regaining the full blessing and favor of God involves a relatively small and simple step.

Where Adam and Eve Went Wrong

When you think of the incredible blessings God gave Adam and Eve in the garden of Eden, it's almost incomprehensible that they would have disobeyed Him and squandered everything. How could that happen?

It all started with subtle deception. The serpent asked a question, implying that God was trying to deprive Adam and Eve of something beneficial: *"Has God indeed said, 'You shall not eat of every tree of the garden'?"* (Genesis 3:1). Notice that he didn't start by directly contradicting the Lord, but he planted a seed of doubt in Eve's mind, so that she questioned God's love and truthfulness. After he had succeeded in planting doubt and distrust in Eve's mind, the serpent was ready to directly challenge what God had said to her. Eve knew God's warning that she and Adam would die if they ate from the Tree of Knowledge of Good and Evil, but the serpent said, *"You will not surely die. For God knows that in the day you eat of it your eyes will be opened, and you will be like God, knowing good and evil"* (Genesis 3:4–5).

There are several important observations we can make in this chilling story. First, it's crucial that we cut off deception in its early stages. The devil is a liar and the father of lies. (See John 8:44.) The more we listen to his lies, the more our deception will grow. That's why we must love the truth of God's Word and use it as a weapon to expose and counteract satan's lies.

Second, the serpent directed Eve's focus to the wrong thing. The account says, *"The tree of life was also in the midst of the garden, and the tree of the knowledge of good and evil"* (Genesis 2:9). You see, there was more than one tree in the middle of the garden, and the primary one was the Tree of Life. But when the serpent focused on the Tree of Knowledge of Good and Evil, Eve began to focus on it, as well. She referred to it as *"the tree which is in the midst of the garden"* (Genesis 3:3), acknowledging that God had forbidden them from eating of it.

Do you see why this subtle shift was so dangerous? The Lord is supposed to be our focus and the center of our lives. The Bible says we should fix our eyes on Him as the Author and Finisher of our faith. (See Hebrews 12:2.) When we shift our attention to anything or to anyone else, we're setting ourselves up for disaster.

Think of it this way: If you have a camera and set the focus on the wrong thing, everything else in the picture will become blurry. Adam and Eve shifted their focus from one tree to another, causing everything to go out of focus. The shift was seemingly small, but the consequences were vast. As the song says, "Jesus, be the center of my life."

Lessons for Leaders

The story of Adam and Eve explains a lot about how leaders—even well-intentioned leaders—can shift their focus off the Lord. In most cases, this is a gradual process and a subtle shift. Like a ship at sea with a broken rudder, there's a slow and steady drift toward dangerous waters.

No Christian leader intends to fail. No pastor intends to leave the ministry due to discouragement or disillusionment. No leader intends to be part of some major scandal. Yet if they don't fix their eyes on Jesus, and if they don't hold on to the nonnegotiable core values of God's kingdom, they're in danger of compromising their convictions when the heat turns on.

We each must be brutally honest with ourselves about our frailties and shortcomings. We must submit those areas of our lives to God and lift them up before the scrutiny of the Holy Spirit. And remember, every private choice has public consequences. What you do behind closed doors will determine the level of God's power, or lack of it, displayed in your public life. And if you're a leader, your private choices will have even *more* of an effect on the lives of others—in either positive or negative ways. Many government, business, and church leaders have learned this lesson the hard way.

You don't have to look very far to find examples of this principle. Remember the Enron scandal? The greedy choices of a few executives affected the corporation and everyone connected with it. Innocent people lost their jobs, their life savings, and their homes because of private choices that had public consequences.

Likewise, Bernie Madoff was a financial advisor who was involved in a Ponzi scheme that brought devastation to countless people. Before his corrupt scheme was exposed, most people thought he was an investment genius, and thousands of people trusted him with their life savings. Billions of dollars were lost because one man put *self* ahead of *service*. Once again, a person's private choices have public consequences and affect innocent people.

I've seen similar tragic stories in my own city, Houston, Texas. Friends and churches sometimes have put their trust in unscrupulous leaders who promised big returns on financial investments. While God can certainly use right alignments and associations to bring about financial blessings and kingdom impact, there will be disastrous results when we put our trust in people of bad character. We need great discernment and wisdom in choosing people to relate to, and we will need even greater discernment in the perilous days ahead.

The Urgency of the Hour

Lou Gerstner was CEO and chairman of IBM when the company faced great challenges and was in drastic need of a major change in the organization's culture. He attributed much of his success to the urgency of his mission:

> Transformation of an enterprise begins with a sense of crisis or urgency. No institution will go through fundamental change unless

it believes it is in deep trouble and needs to do something different to survive.[1]

When he spoke these words at the Harvard Business School, Gerstner was primarily referring to the transformation of IBM, but the same principle applies to any kind of transformational leadership. If we're going to see transformational change in the institutions and organizations of our times, we must recognize their desperate need for change, and we must communicate that urgency to everyone involved.

The Bible describes this as a key leadership trait in *"the sons of Issachar who had understanding of the times, to know what Israel ought to do"* (1 Chronicles 12:32). Before we can transform the culture of a company, a church, a family, or a nation, we must understand the times in which we live. We then must seek God's wisdom for what we ought to do to bring about deep and lasting change.

You see, transformational leaders recognize the necessity of laying strong, deep foundations. Why? Because we're told in Scripture that there will be a great shaking on the earth. (See Hebrews 12:25–28.) We're warned to build our lives and our organizations upon God's eternal kingdom, *"which cannot be shaken"* (Hebrews 12:27).

If your life has undergone a great shaking in recent years, you shouldn't really be surprised. Everything people lean upon for their safety and security will be shaken—institutions, organizations, families, finances—nothing is exempt.

The Bible speaks of how this shaking will impact even the natural realm: *"We know that the whole creation groans and labors with birth pangs together until now"* (Romans 8:22). In recent decades, we've seen an increase in the number and intensity of natural disasters, such as earthquakes, tornadoes, forest fires, tsunamis, and other kinds of *"birth pangs."* In addition, there has been an increase in terrorism and political unrest. Transformational leaders must recognize such signs of the times, while never forgetting that God still sits on the throne of heaven:

---

1. Lou Gerstner in a talk to students at Harvard Business School, Martha Lagace, *Gerstner: Changing Culture at IBM – Lou Gerstner Discusses Changing the Culture at IBM*, December 9, 2002, http://hbswk.hbs.edu/archive/3209.html.

Why do the nations rage, and the people plot a vain thing? The kings of the earth set themselves, and the rulers take counsel together, against the LORD *and against His Anointed, saying, "Let us break Their bonds in pieces and cast away Their cords from us." He who sits in the heavens shall laugh; the Lord shall hold them in derision. Then He shall speak to them in His wrath, and distress them in His deep displeasure: "Yet I have set My King On My holy hill of Zion."*   (Psalm 2:1–6)

Like Queen Esther, you and I have been called into God's kingdom *"for such a time as this"* (Esther 4:14). While everything around us is being shaken, we're called to be persevering, courageous, transformational leaders who will equip the Lord's people for these perilous times. (See 2 Timothy 3:1.)

Not only does God want us to finish well as leaders, but He also wants us to prepare His people to finish well in their own lives.

To grant us that we, being delivered from the hand of our enemies, might serve Him without fear, in holiness and righteousness before Him all the days of our life.   (Luke 1:74–75)

We live in an age of unprecedented challenge and unparalleled opportunity. Our hope is not in the institutions of men, political parties, a man or woman, or our personal preferences or opinions, but in our Lord, the Hope of Glory.

3

Exposing the Hidden Things

What Eleanor Roosevelt said of women is true of all of us: "A woman is like a tea bag—you can't tell how strong she is until you put her in hot water." I have seen that principle played out in my own life and in the lives of many other Christian leaders.

When trials come or adversaries rise up against us, God often uses it as an opportunity to expose areas of sin, error, or presumption in our lives. King David wisely cried out to the Lord to free him from any destructive forces lurking in his heart:

Who can understand his errors? Cleanse me from secret faults. Keep back Your servant also from presumptuous sins; let them not have dominion over me. Then I shall be blameless, and I shall be innocent of great transgression. Let the words of my mouth and the meditation of my heart be acceptable in Your sight, O LORD, my strength and my Redeemer. (Psalm 19:12–14)

And notice how proactive David was in asking God to search his heart:

Search me, O God, and know my heart; test me and know my anxious thoughts. Point out anything in me that offends you, and lead me along the path of everlasting life. (Psalm 139:23–24 NLT)

Of course, there are a variety of ways God can answer this prayer and reveal our hearts. We can be convicted of sin as we read His Word or His

Spirit can speak to us during our prayer times. At other times, adversity or criticism serves as a refiner's fire, bringing out the impurities so we can shine like pure gold. (See Job 23:10.)

I've also found that time, like light, is often used by the Lord to manifest truth. Given enough time, an individual's true character is revealed. And as time goes on, we often can outlive our difficult circumstances and outlast our adversaries. Every adversity is an opportunity for God to show Himself even greater.

Pressure Magnifies

One of the outstanding principles I learned from Dr. Edwin Louis Cole is that pressure magnifies. One of the examples he gave was of a baseball player up to bat in the ninth inning of the first game of the season with bases loaded. It's a pretty big deal whether he hits a grand slam or strikes out. However, it's a far *bigger* deal if he's in the seventh game of the World Series. There's a lot more pressure at a time like that, and everyone will remember his success or failure at that moment far more than his performance in the first game of the year.

Dr. Cole's axiom is especially relevant today, when we're living in a time of great pressure throughout the world. Leaders are finding themselves surrounded by pressure-cooker situations. It's crucial at such times to learn how to walk in the Spirit of God rather than allow ourselves to react according to the dictates of our flesh. (See Galatians 5:16–26.)

Furthermore, pressure magnifies both the good and

PROVOKE-A-THOUGHT:

"TIME IS A PRECIOUS COMMODITY. ONCE IT IS USED, IT CANNOT BE RETRIEVED. WITH SO MUCH TO DO, YET SO LITTLE TIME, MAKE SURE TO MAKE THE BEST OF YOUR TIME."

the evil qualities in our lives. It tests us, enabling us to see in vivid color what our core values are. We learn whether we've truly embraced the non-negotiable principles of God's Word. In these times, when the pressures of life seem unbearable and overwhelming, where can we turn? King David said it well:

> *Hear my cry, O God; attend to my prayer. From the end of the earth I will cry to You, when my heart is overwhelmed; lead me to the rock that is higher than I. For You have been a shelter for me, a strong tower from the enemy. I will abide in Your tabernacle forever; I will trust in the shelter of Your wings.*   (Psalm 61:1–4)

Sometimes our human strength and resources simply run dry. I periodically find myself praying, "Lord, help me to draw from the well You've given me—the well that never runs dry, because its Source never ceases."

You see, it's important to have your core values and nonnegotiables in place *before* the pressures of life reach the critical stage. You need to establish your source of Living Water, because your earthly resources are likely to run dry. Yes, sometimes you may feel really dry, but you can find comfort in the water Source that never ceases.

The Question of Consistency

When Mike Rosas, a chaplain of the Houston Rockets basketball team, asked me to mentor him, he initially said, "Doug, I've followed your ministry for many years and have been struck by your consistency to your vision and purpose. How are you able to be so consistent?"

I chuckled and replied, "If you would like, I can tell you all the bad things about me. Maybe that would help to put things into perspective."

"No, no. I don't need you to tell me anything like that," he said.

"To be honest, the answer is that I can stand only by the grace of God," I explained. "But there are foundational value systems that I've applied since my early years of ministry as a young single man in my twenties." I went on to describe how quickly I'd discovered my vulnerabilities in those early years. I had been all guy and had lots of pent-up energy. I had gone

PROVOKE-A-THOUGHT:

"BE CAREFUL NOT TO LET THE 'MACHINE' OF YOUR LIFE OR MINISTRY RULE THE MINISTER. BE HONEST WITH YOURSELF, RECOGNIZE YOUR AREAS OF WEAKNESS AND VULNERABILITY, AND THEN SET PROTECTIVE PARAMETERS."

into ministry thinking I could lasso the moon. Hey, I had God on my side, so I was sure that nothing would be impossible for me.

However, I told Mike about the rude awakening I experienced when God revealed my weaknesses to me. I had to be brutally honest with myself and recognize my human weaknesses. In addition to learning to be accountable to the Lord in these matters, I discovered that I must set parameters and policies to help reduce temptations. I also needed to surround myself with godly people I could lean on and draw from, people who would keep me personally accountable.

If you've begun to discover your character flaws and weaknesses, don't despair. God can help you and give you the resources you need to walk in victory, as Paul assured the Corinthians:

No temptation has overtaken you except such as is common to man; but God is faithful, who will not allow you to be tempted beyond what you are able, but with the temptation will also make the way of escape, that you may be able to bear it. (1 Corinthians 10:13)

What a great message this is! Yes, there will be temptations for each of us. But we can take courage that God is faithful, and He will always provide a way of escape when we seek Him.

During my first ten years of ministry, I had loads of passion and great love for God, yet I was frequently faced with my human frailty and flaws. Time and again, I was reminded that I stood only by God's grace, and over and over, I cried out to the Lord, "Without You, I am nothing!" (See 1 Corinthians 15:10.)

So you see why I was mildly amused when the Houston Rockets' chaplain asked me about the secret to my consistency. There was nothing quick or automatic about that trait in my life. It came through a gradual process of growing in the Lord and learning to rely upon His grace and power.

My experience is reflected in the beloved old hymn "I Need Thee Every Hour" by Annie S. Hawks and Robert Lowry:

I need Thee every hour, most gracious Lord;
No tender voice like Thine can peace afford.
Refrain: I need Thee, O I need Thee;
Every hour I need Thee;
O bless me now, my Savior, I come to Thee.

I need Thee every hour, stay Thou nearby;
Temptations lose their power when Thou art nigh.
(Refrain)

I need Thee every hour, in joy or pain;
Come quickly and abide, or life is in vain.
(Refrain)

I need Thee every hour; teach me Thy will;
And Thy rich promises in me fulfill.
(Refrain)

I need Thee every hour, most Holy One;
O make me Thine indeed, Thou blessed Son.
(Refrain)[2]

If you are struggling in some area of your life, I hope you will remember the words of this beautiful hymn. You need the Lord! You never were meant to live the Christian life in your own strength. The key to victory is Christ living His life through you. (See Galatians 2:20; Colossians 1:27.)

---

2. Annie S. Hawks and Robert Lowry, "I Need Thee Every Hour," 1872.

Laying a Firm Foundation

The Bible has a lot to say about roots and foundations. Why? Though both roots and foundations are hidden underground, they are absolutely vital to what happens aboveground. No wonder Jesus said we would need to *dig deep* in order to build our lives upon solid rock. (See Luke 6:48.) Storms and trials will always test the foundation our lives are built upon. No matter your specific calling and focus as a Christian leader, the only way to guarantee sustainable, long-term fruitfulness and blessing is to make sure you build on the right foundation.

This was Paul's message in 1 Corinthians 3:11: *"No other foundation can anyone lay than that which is laid, which is Jesus Christ."* This principle applies not just to the foundation of the church but to anything else you attempt to build. Your business, your home, your ministry, and so forth must be built upon the indestructible foundation of Jesus Christ and aligned with God's kingdom.

My mother was Japanese and my father and stepfather were both from Texas and served in the U.S. Navy. She came to live with me in Houston for eight years after becoming widowed. One day as I was walking out the door to go speak at a prayer conference, she said with considerable urgency, "Dougie, you got to do something about the cracks in the wall."

"Okay," I responded, but my mother persisted.

"Cracks in the wall mean something go wrong with foundation. If you don't fix foundation, then more cracks in the wall and maybe plumbing and everything else go bad. You got to fix!"

"Mother, okay, I see what you are saying, but I can't do anything right now. I'm going to speak at a conference with Jim Cymbala and Jack Hayford."

I thought my mother would recognize how important the prayer conference was, but she seemed much more concerned about the foundation of my house.

Mama was right in her concern. The shifting of my foundation was messing up the rest of the house, causing a misalignment that would inevitably cause more problems later. Sadly, I neglected to get the foundation fixed even after my mother's exhortation. And sure enough, the cracks grew, the plumbing was compromised, and the damage cost me a lot more than it would have cost if I'd gotten it fixed right away.

Although this neglect was costly, it can be even more costly when Christians neglect their spiritual foundations. We've got to build on the firm foundation of Christ and the enduring principles of His kingdom. Everything else will be shaken and shattered, but the kingdom of God will remain. (See Hebrews 12:25–29.)

PROVOKE-A-THOUGHT:

"WE WILL COME TO OUR KNEES BY CHOICE OR BY CIRCUMSTANCE."

Take a moment right now to allow the Holy Spirit to examine your life. Are there some cracks in the walls of your life, early warning signs that your foundation is askew? Are there blind spots or areas of vulnerability you need to address in order to prevent a collapse down the road?

Storm-Proofing Your Life

As a child, you probably heard the famous story "The Three Little Pigs." The first pig built a house of straw, but the big bad wolf came and easily blew it down. The second pig tried a slightly different approach and built his house with sticks. However, the result was the same. The wolf blew the house down. The third pig was wiser than his hapless friends. He took the time and expense to build a house out of bricks. The big bad wolf soon came and, just as he had done with the others, he huffed and puffed, but the house made of bricks withstood the test.

I love how the story ends. Unable to blow down the brick house, the wolf goes down the chimney. Yet the pig had been farsighted enough to build a fire in the fireplace, complete with a cauldron of boiling water. When the wolf fell into the cauldron, the pig quickly slammed a lid over it and cooked the wolf, which soon became a tasty dinner.

This story has resonated in people's hearts for more than a century, because it contains two vital truths. First, in order to withstand the enemy's attacks, we must have a solid foundation and durable building materials. Second, we must ensure that we keep a *fire* in our spiritual fireplace. Unless we maintain a burning passion for the Lord, the enemy can sneak down our chimney!

The story of the pigs is actually a reflection of the story Jesus told about two men who built two houses, one on sand and the other on rock. (See Matthew 7:24–27; Luke 6:46–49.) Other than their foundations, both houses were probably identical, looking very impressive and enviable on the outside. But everything changed when storm winds and floods came, testing the durability of the men's construction. The house of the man who had taken time to dig deep and lay a solid foundation survived, but the house built on a superficial, sandy foundation was destroyed.

"Cosmetic" Christianity

Dr. Cole used to warn against "cosmetic" Christianity—religiosity that looks good on the surface but lacks substance and durability. Like costume jewelry, it may look good on the outside, but it will never match the value of the real thing. As Dr. Cole used to say, this kind of empty spirituality is "high gloss, cheap merchandise."

Why is it that so few Christian leaders seem to take time to dig deep and build their lives on solid rock instead of shifting sand? Living on shifting sand may work for a while, but when a storm comes, their lives will be shattered.

Being from Houston, I know a few things about storms. Hurricanes, tornadoes, tropical storms, and floods—we've seen it all down here. So we are well aware of the urgency of laying a firm foundation *before* the storm clouds form.

I'll never forget the devastation caused by the Haitian earthquake in 2010. A magnitude 7.0 earthquake can cause considerable damage even under the best of circumstances. But the situation in Haiti was catastrophic, because most homes and buildings had been built on faulty foundations.

They didn't just *crack* under the stress of the earthquake, they *collapsed*. As a result, more than 100,000 people were killed.

This is no time for fair-weather Christianity. The earth is groaning, and everything that can be shaken *will* be shaken. The nations are raging. The heat is rising. Like never before, we need bold, courageous leaders whose lives are built on the steadfast foundation of Christ.

You have been called into God's kingdom *"for such a time as this"* (Esther 4:14). Instead of shrinking back from the Lord's purpose for your life, you will need courage and perseverance to face the challenges ahead.

> *You need to persevere so that when you have done the will of God, you will receive what he has promised. For, "In just a little while, he who is coming will come and will not delay." And, "But my righteous one will live by faith. And I take no pleasure in the one who shrinks back." But we do not belong to those who shrink back and are destroyed, but to those who have faith and are saved.* (Hebrews 10:36–39 NIV)

If you've taken time to build your life on a solid foundation, you have nothing to fear from the storms of life. Even if the devil knocks on your door as a "big bad wolf," your house will stand strong and triumphant.

4

United for a Purpose

Once we've aligned ourselves with God's kingdom and the precepts of His Word, it's crucial that we also come into right alignment with the people He wants us to associate with. This sounds easy enough, but often it's not. Alignment with the wrong people can be very costly, while proper unity with godly comrades releases great blessings. (See Psalm 133:1–3.)

Too often, people think that unity and alignment are gained simply by joining some organization, denomination, or club. But biblical unity is much more than that; it's unity with a purpose—a kingdom purpose. Biblical unity begins when we recognize that there is *"one body"* of Christ followers, and that we're called to maintain *"the unity of the Spirit in the bond of peace"* (Ephesians 4:3). But the process of unity and alignment is meant to continue until we are *"joined and knit together by what every joint supplies, according to the effective working by which every part does its share"* (Ephesians 4:16). Notice that unity is not the same as uniformity, for every part is designed to fulfill a distinct and unique role that contributes to the common good. (See 1 Corinthians 12:7; 1 Peter 4:10–11.)

God wants the body of Christ to be more than just a pile of random body parts. When we allow that to happen, we inevitably become a valley of dry bones, like Ezekiel's vision of the scattered nation of Israel. (See Ezekiel 37:1–14.) But just as we see in that stirring vision, God wants to bring us together, *"bone to bone"* (verse 7), and then breathe new life into us with the ultimate purpose of making us *"an exceedingly great army"* (Ezekiel 37:10) that can reach the world for Jesus.

Just as Israel was one nation with twelve tribes, the church of Christ is one body with many "tribes." Yes, we have *"one Lord, one faith, one baptism; one God and Father of all"* (Ephesians 4:5–6), but we are called to function in different parts of the body.

Do you know what tribe you're a part of in God's kingdom? Are you linked with other believers of like mind and vision in a functional way, working together to impact the world for Christ? Clarity of your proper alignment will save you lots of distress and frustration.

Commitment and Clarity

We live in a culture where commitments and agreements are often shallow and unreliable. It used to be that bonds were formed through a handshake or verbal promise. But today, you can't count on a person's promise unless you have it in writing—and even then you may wonder if he or she will actually follow through.

Have you ever had to read all the legalese in your agreement with your insurance company to make sure they weren't ripping you off? Perhaps they didn't tell you about all the exclusions of coverage, such as flood damage. And isn't it interesting that most product-warranty disclaimers and exclusions are written in fine print, difficult to read without a magnifying glass?

Throughout my years of ministry, I've learned that agreements with others must be based on clear communication. We can't just *assume* we're in agreement when partnering with someone on a project. Nor can we leave room for false expectations. Sometimes this requires putting the plan or agreement in writing, not out of distrust but simply for the sake of clarity. Even God Himself knew our need to put our visions into writing: *"Write the vision and make it plain on tablets, that he may run who reads it"* (Habakkuk 2:2). Clarity of vision and clarity of agreement go hand in hand, minimizing conflict and maximizing unity and effectiveness.

Kindred Hearts

The apostle Paul pointed out that some of his coworkers were more like-minded than others:

I hope in the Lord Jesus to send Timothy to you shortly, so that I also may be encouraged when I learn of your condition. For I have no one else of kindred spirit who will genuinely be concerned for your welfare.
(Philippians 2:19–20 NASB)

Isn't this a fascinating statement? Of all the people Paul could have sent to help the Philippians, he said that Timothy was uniquely qualified for the task, for he was *"of kindred spirit."*

True unity is a matter of two or more people having the same heart, spirit, and purpose. (See Ephesians 4:3.) That means that we don't just share the same doctrines or opinions on the correct organizational structure. We can unite two cats by tying their tails together, but that certainly doesn't ensure unity or proper alignment.

Genuine unity occurs when there is common vision and a clear understanding of who God has put in charge of leading a team. It never works when there's a fuzzy vision or multiple people battling for leadership. The Lord brings harmony when there is a mutual bond of love and submission, everyone knowing his or her role and deferring to one another in proper alignment.

Before I continue, take a moment to pray and ask yourself whether you truly have unity of heart and spirit with the main people you relate to in life, business, or ministry. Is there godly affection and warmth in your marriage, and in relationships with your children and leadership teams at your company, nonprofit organization, or church? If not, now is a great time to drop to your knees and ask God for a turnaround. First, let Him change *your* heart, and then invite Him to transform your relationships, as well.

Servanthood or Sedition?

Too often, a person is placed into a position of leadership based on his or her personality, family connections, financial success, or some other misguided reason. Other times, a person is hired into a business or ministry role because he or she seems fit to meet some desperate need in the organization, even when the position doesn't really match his or her calling or gifting. We must wait for, and groom, the right people for the right positions.

The Bible provides many examples of toxic and seditious leaders. In Scripture, sedition is anything that undermines God's constituted authority. This is the exact opposite of the fundamental biblical principle of leadership. In order to exercise valid authority, people must be under our authority. Even Jesus, the Son of God, was under authority, as the Roman centurion wisely recognized. (See Luke 7:2–10.)

In contrast, seditious leaders actively try to undermine God's constituted authority. One of the clearest examples of this is David's son Absalom:

> *Absalom would rise early and stand beside the way to the gate. So it was, whenever anyone who had a lawsuit came to the king for a decision, that Absalom would call to him and say, "What city are you from?" And he would say, "Your servant is from such and such a tribe of Israel." Then Absalom would say to him, "Look, your case is good and right; but there is no deputy of the king to hear you." Moreover Absalom would say, "Oh, that I were made judge in the land, and everyone who has any suit or cause would come to me; then I would give him justice." And so it was, whenever anyone came near to bow down to him, that he would put out his hand and take him and kiss him. In this manner Absalom acted toward all Israel who came to the king for judgment. So Absalom stole the hearts of the men of Israel.* (2 Samuel 15:2–6)

The last line of this passage is chilling, isn't it? *"Absalom **stole the hearts** of the men of Israel."* He was a tragic example of someone who did everything he could to undercut his father's goodwill (and, in this case, his kingdom) by spreading dissension and disunity. Sadly, this reality is experienced at one time or another by almost every Christian leader. You are bound to face some Absaloms—ambitious people not under authority—who will try to undercut your authority.

Queen Jezebel was another toxic leader. Although she had "positional" authority—carrying the title of queen—she didn't have true authority that comes only from being submitted to God and His purposes. This self-centered, narcissistic leader actively tried to undermine the prophets of the Lord.

What is the best way to counteract seditious leaders like Absalom and Jezebel? First of all, we need to make sure we are operating under God's authority. If we have submitted our lives fully to the Lord, we will move God's authority and favor, and we will be able to rebuke not only toxic leaders but even the devil himself. (See James 4:7.)

Curing Leadership Dysfunctions

I've been on the board of a number of organizations, and a few of them have been pretty dysfunctional. Often I've found that founders of an organization begin with great passion and vision but don't properly impart that vision to their board members or to the next generation of leaders. Sometimes, there are remnants of the original vision, but things become institutional rather than organic and dynamic. The organization may do some good things, but it's just a shell of what it once was. It requires more and more money but has diminishing results.

Once an organization becomes institutional rather than visionary, it becomes harder and harder to attract donors, volunteers, or even employees. Why? Because people are attracted to vision more than to need. If your organization has lost its passion and is constantly groveling for money, don't be surprised if people don't respond. They want their stewardship to count, so they give to vision, not to need alone.

Effective church and nonprofit leaders realize the importance of gratitude. They don't just beat the drum and say, "Gimme, gimme, send me money to serve my vision." We must treat people as true partners in the ministry, and constantly thank them for their faithful support. Remember the great story of Jesus healing ten lepers, only one of whom returned to say thanks? (See Luke 17:11–19.)

In the final analysis, there's one critical difference between effective leaders and seditious ones. Effective leaders recognize their role as servants and are willing to wash people's feet as an example to others (see John 13:1–17); in contrast, toxic or seditious leaders are always trying to build their own kingdom and serve themselves. They are all about their own title, power, and position, and they know very little about empowering others or forming an effective team.

PROVOKE-A-THOUGHT:

"WHILE MEN REACH FOR THRONES TO BUILD THEIR OWN KINGDOMS, JESUS REACHED FOR A TOWEL TO WASH MEN'S FEET."

No matter what leadership position you're in, you need to rid yourself of the perspective that everybody should be serving you. Instead of craving an exalted place for yourself, dwell on Jesus the exalted One, who holds the highest place of all. Rather than being like so many leaders who reach for thrones to build their kingdoms, be like our Lord Jesus, who reached for a towel to wash people's feet.

Author Richard Foster writes, "As the Cross is the sign of submission, so the towel is the sign of service.... Jesus took a towel and basin and redefined greatness."[3] Do you aspire to greatness? Are you looking for lasting success? Then follow the pathway Jesus prescribed:

> You know that the rulers of the Gentiles lord it over them, and those who are great exercise authority over them. Yet it shall not be so among you; but whoever desires to become great among you, let him be your servant. And whoever desires to be first among you, let him be your slave—just as the Son of Man did not come to be served, but to serve, and to give His life a ransom for many.   (Matthew 20:25–28)

---

3. Richard J. Foster, *Celebration of Discipline: The Path to Spiritual Growth* (San Francisco, CA: Harper Collins Publishers, 1988), 126.

This servanthood principle applies to everyone. It applies just the same to a waitress, a small business owner, a factory worker, and a preacher. When you sincerely serve people with your message, your product, or your good service, you are likely to receive a positive response. If you display a servant's heart and build authentic relationships, those you influence will gladly tell others about your business, product, or church. On the other hand, you'll seldom fool people if you're serving them only as a means to your own selfish ends.

PROVOKE-A-THOUGHT:

"WHILE WE PURSUE EXALTED AND HIGH PLACES, JESUS, THE EXALTED ONE, LEFT HIS HIGHEST PLACE TO PURSUE US."

There's an unavoidable reality to true servanthood: You have to die to yourself! This is not merely a *principle* of leadership; it's a foundational *requirement* of discipleship. (See Luke 9:23; John 12:24.) As Dietrich Bonhoeffer said, "When Christ calls a man, he bids him come and die."[4]

Leadership Structures

In order to be as effective as possible, I believe an organization should have structural order and infrastructures. However, it's not healthy when a church, ministry, or company exalts titles above service. I believe that God calls some people to be apostles, prophets, bishops, bosses, and CEOs, but things get out of balance when the structures and titles of those positions outpace the service and functions.

The skeleton gives the human body a structure. Without it, we would be just a glob of organs, skin, and soft tissue that would accomplish very little. In many ways, leadership provides structure, too; however, although leaders are necessary, they are not supposed to be preeminent! To the contrary, they are called to provide *support* for the rest of the organization.

4. Dietrich Bonhoeffer, *The Cost of Discipleship* (New York, NY: Touchstone, 1959, 1995), 89.

Yet, as it was in Bible times so it is today—inevitably there are leaders like Diotrephes, who cause problems because they seek *"preeminence"* (3 John 1:9) instead of godly influence through servanthood.

Remember, the church is the greatest and most successful enterprise of all time. The secret to its success has not been its leadership structures or fancy titles, but rather its ability to bring about an incarnational impartation of God's presence. The infrastructures clearly didn't come first but developed along the way to handle something God was doing by His Spirit.

"But Doug," you may want to protest, "the Bible says that the church was built upon *'the foundation of the apostles and prophets'* (Ephesians 2:20). Doesn't that show the importance of strong leadership?"

The answer is yes and no. Surely there was strong leadership in the early church. However, the apostles and prophets were part of the *foundation*. This was not top-down leadership as we might envision it today. Instead, these leaders laid down their lives as servants of the Lord, for His kingdom and for His people. They made sacrifices and paid a price, selflessly denying themselves and picking up the Cross of Christ. (See Luke 9:23.) They did not exalt themselves but laid down their lives to equip and empower others for the work of ministry. (See Ephesians 4:11–12.)

PROVOKE-A-THOUGHT:

"FROM PREACHERS TO POLITICIANS, PULPITS TO POLITICAL OFFICES, WE NEED A REVIVAL OF CHARACTER AND COURAGEOUS LEADERSHIP."

Good leaders should not be lids that hold people down but rather stepladders that lift people up. We're to encourage and empower people, equipping them to fulfill their God-given vision. As you devote yourself to helping others fulfill *their* vision, they often will become the very ones to help you expand *your* vision.

5

Credibility and Associations

No matter what area of leadership God has called you to, your credibility will be a key factor in how much influence you really have. Leaders with low credibility will have a low level of influence—it's just that simple.

Solomon wrote, *"A good name is to be more desired than great wealth, favor is better than silver and gold"* (Proverbs 22:1 NASB). A good reputation was so important that it was deemed one of the requirements for leadership in the early church. (See Acts 6:3; 1 Timothy 3:2, 7; 5:9–10; Titus 1:6.) When accused and defamed, the apostle Paul was quick to point out that he was an honorable and trustworthy man. (See Acts 20:18–20; 2 Corinthians 2:17; 8:21; 1 Thessalonians 2:1–12.)

PROVOKE-A-THOUGHT:

"THE BIBLE IS FILLED WITH STORIES OF HEROIC BELIEVERS WHO OBEYED GOD AND DID MIGHTY EXPLOITS IN DIFFICULT SITUATIONS. WE ARE TOLD TO CONSIDER THEIR FAITH AND IMITATE THEIR MANNER OF LIFE."

One of the uncontestable facts of life and leadership is that people will often judge a leader's credibility partly based on whom he associates with. As early as the sixteenth century, an English proverb stated, "Birds of a feather flock together," and people instinctively take this as a rule of thumb today.

There's no doubt about it, if you tell me who your closest friends and associates are, I can tell you a lot about your character and your prospects for success. The Bible clearly says, "*He who walks with wise men will be wise, but the companion of fools will be destroyed*" (Proverbs 13:20). In contrast, "*Bad company corrupts good character*" (1 Corinthians 15:33 niv).

You see, the warning to not to be "*unequally yoked*" (2 Corinthians 6:14–18) doesn't apply just to our choice of a marriage partner. It also applies to our friendships, associations, career choices, business partners, and ministry relationships.

Detecting Opportunists

If you are in any type of leadership role, some people will try to associate with you to enhance their credibility. Over the decades, I've had many people say they that felt called to work with me, but later I realized that they were just looking for a stepping-stone to something else they were after. It made me feel used.

How do you respond to people who try to associate with you to further their own ambitions? I've determined not to take offense in such situations, but to bless those who've used me. Jesus said to "*pray for those who spitefully use you*" (Luke 6:28), and that is what I endeavor to do. I pray something like this: "Lord, I bless them anyway. Whatever people or organizations have used our ministry as a stepping-stone, I pray that they will get closer to You, and I ask You to bless their socks off."

I'll never forget one of the funniest examples of someone who tried to associate with me to gain credibility. I was at a worship gathering, and a man walked up to me and started a conversation.

"What group are you with?" he asked.

"I'm a part of Somebody Cares," I told him.

"Oh! Somebody Cares! You're with Doug Stringer. He's a good friend of mine," the man said.

"Really?" I replied.

It was a very awkward moment for this young man, and I felt embarrassed for him when he asked, "What's your name?"

"I'm Doug Stringer," I informed him.

"Oh, did you shave or something? Or maybe cut your hair?"

"Yeah, it must be something like that," I said with a slight grin.

You see, this man thought he could gain some kind of credibility and access by saying he knew me. Many of us do even worse when we try to fake association with the Lord. We want to use His name or a few Bible references or the name of some church to gain access or credibility. Countless recording artists started singing in church but aren't living for the Lord today. And you've probably encountered people who networked with Christians just to expand their business or political campaign.

Yes, people will attempt to use you, your ministry, your church, or your business to advance their own agenda, credibility, or platform. But if you remain sensitive to God's Spirit, He will help you recognize what is happening before any significant damage is done.

As you move into new higher levels of influence, you will need an even greater discernment of the people who want to have a relationship with you. Some will say they want to serve you; others will flatter you by saying that they want you to be their mentor or spiritual father or mother. I hear such things all the time. But how should we respond?

Years ago, I would have been more prone to automatically say yes to such overtures, but my approach has changed. Typically I'll say, "Look, let's not put any labels on any kind of relationship yet. Can we just journey together for a while? We'll know when God works out our relationship in time. But for now, let's just walk this out as fellow believers in the Lord, helping each other grow in Christ. Perhaps God will add a title or label to our relationship in time, but that's not really His main priority."

Where Are the Godly Mentors?

I've found that most leaders in my generation really struggle to be spiritual fathers or mothers, even when they believe the relationship is one that has been divinely orchestrated. Why? Because few of them have had that kind of relationship in their own lives, whether in a nuclear family or in a ministry.

I've had some interesting experiences as I've endeavored to make myself available to young leaders in the next generation. "Doug, we're not asking you to be perfect or to tell us what to do," they often tell me. "We're not putting any big expectations on you. We just want to be connected and associated with you as we journey through life." More than anything else, they seem to be craving authenticity. Years ago, people were often dazzled by a leader's spiritual gifts; but today, young people are more impressed if a leader knows how to be a genuine friend to them.

Sadly, many people in ministry are still "Lone Rangers." Instead of benefiting from the associations and alignments God wants to give them, they remain aloof and isolated. Because of their independence and refusal to bond with other leaders, they are putting themselves in great jeopardy. Some people are in danger because of their detachment from the body of Christ, while others are *"covenantbreakers"* (Romans 1:31 KJV)—forming commitments they don't keep.

Friend, I hope you recognize that healthy relationships are vitally important to our success and longevity as leaders. They define our destinies, and they are critical if we want to finish well in the race of life. Years ago, I concluded that I never would have achieved what I achieved without the help of lots of people. Some people mentored me and poured their life into me when I was still a young leader. Others made incredible sacrifices in partnering with me to reach lost and broken people with the gospel of Christ.

Furthermore, I've learned that it's not enough just to feel gratitude for the people who have helped me along the way; I must also express that gratitude and appreciation, showing them honor in tangible, public ways.

Give Honor to Whom Honor Is Due

Paul wrote to the Romans to give *"honor to whom honor is due"* (Romans 13:7 RSV). Honoring our leaders is indispensable if we want to maximize God's blessings and favor in our lives, but it is often neglected in our culture today. In fact, honor and respect are often replaced with a critical spirit.

I hope you're actively looking for ways to honor the people around you. If you're not used to doing that, it may take a while to incorporate it into your lifestyle. But when you learn to sow honor, you will reap honor, as well.

We live in a world of people who compete for position or status, trying to climb the corporate ladder or get a bigger platform for their ministry or achieve greater financial success. Instead of pursuing selfish ambitions, we all should aspire to *"outdo one another in showing honor"* (Romans 12:10 ESV). And I love how *The Message* paraphrases this: *"Practice playing second fiddle."*

Showing honor was put into perspective for me several years ago, when I was selected to receive the Barbara Jordan Leadership Award. I had been nominated by the Houston Police Department, and the presentation was to be held at the Hyatt Regency downtown. It was a black-tie affair, taking me totally out of my comfort zone. I had to buy a black suit and white dress shirt for the event. All the major media attended the event, as well as representatives from the mayor's office. It was a rather intimidating experience for a street preacher like me, someone who is more used to hanging out with the homeless, drug addicts, and prostitutes.

When they finally called me up to receive the award, I said, "Look, I can't take credit for this myself. I first want to thank the Lord, because there's no way I would be doing what I do today if it weren't for what He's done in my life."

I wanted to make sure I gave glory to God, but I also wanted to acknowledge the wonderful friends and volunteers who helped make Somebody Cares happen. "There are so many people who deserve to be here more than I do," I said at the podium. "I don't even deserve to be here, but I'm receiving this award on behalf of many other people who have worked together to touch people's lives."

You see, even if you are honored for some successful ministry or business, it's not just about you. It's an honor received on behalf of those you're associated with, or your co-laborers. And, ultimately, it's all about advancing the purposes of God and equipping people to fulfill their vision and destiny.

After the awards event, I was a nervous wreck. I was waiting for the valet to bring my car, when someone from the mayor's office walked by and asked, "Hey, do you know Minnie Pearl?"

At that moment, I couldn't even remember who Minnie Pearl was. Later, I remembered that she was a character on the old *Hee Haw* television comedy show, and her trademark was leaving price tags on all of her hats and clothes.

When I got back to my apartment, I finally figured out why that man had asked me about Minnie Pearl. As I took off the new black suit, I discovered that the price tag was still hanging from underneath the arm! Knowing I was prone to getting big-headed about the honor I received, God used this to keep me humble—I had been filmed by Houston's best news media accepting an award with a price tag hanging from my clothes!

> **PROVOKE-A-THOUGHT:**
>
> "CREDIBILITY AND ACCESS IS OFTEN GAINED BY ASSOCIATION. NEVER FORGET TO APPRECIATE WHERE YOU CAME FROM AND THOSE WHO LENT YOU THEIR CREDIBILITY ALONG THE WAY."

New Levels, New Devils

You have to be careful when you move into new levels of influence. As some preachers like to point out, "With new levels, you face new devils." I encourage you to take some time to study 1 Peter 5:1–11 because it provides a wonderful outline of the kinds of temptations leaders are bound to face along the way. Peter warns against such things as dishonesty, greed, lording over people, and spiritual pride.

Peter advises leaders to clothe themselves with humility, for *"God resists the proud, but gives grace to the humble"* (1 Peter 5:5). *"Clothed with humility"* (verse 5) accurately describes Jesus when He washed Peter's feet in John 13. The *Amplified Bible* renders this phrase *"tie on the servant's apron"* (1 Peter 5:5 AMP), a beautiful word picture of the nature of true leadership.

Peter goes on to say that if we've humbled ourselves under the mighty hand of God, He will exalt us *"in due time"* (1 Peter 5:6). Isn't it good to know that there's no need to exalt ourselves? Nor is there any hurry, for He knows the times and seasons in our lives. Instead of sweating the challenges of life or ministry, we can cast every care upon Him, knowing that He cares for us. (See verse 7.)

This section of Scripture then provides some instructions for how you can gain victory over *"your adversary the devil"* (verse 8), and it ends with a powerful reminder that our life and ministry must be devoted to God's glory rather than to our own: *"To Him be the glory and the dominion forever and ever. Amen"* (verse 11).

Sometimes, people act as if it's a great mystery why so many leaders don't finish well in their life and ministry. Peter's exhortation offers some of the best reasons, and he also tells us how we can guard ourselves from satan's snares and the pitfalls of life. Amazingly, though centuries have passed since these words were written, they are still just as applicable to the hazards Christian leaders face today.

PROVOKE-A-THOUGHT:

"IF WE ARE TO FINISH WELL, WE SHOULD CONSIDER THE IMPORTANCE OF OUR SPIRITUAL, PHYSICAL, AND EMOTIONAL HEALTH."

6

The Folly of Going It Alone

Pastor and author Joe McKeever pointed out that one of the traits of people who finish well is that they understand their need for other believers. Instead of going it alone, they draw on the encouragement, support, and accountability of their brothers and sisters in Christ.

McKeever says that too many Christian leaders are like young children who say, "I can do it myself, Mom!" Pastors, he says, are notorious for their Lone Ranger-approach to ministry, which often brings tragic results.

The writer of Hebrews describes why this issue is so important:

Take care, brethren, that there not be in any one of you an evil, unbelieving heart that falls away from the living God. But encourage one another day after day, as long as it is still called "Today," so that none of you will be hardened by the deceitfulness of sin.
(Hebrews 3:12–13 NASB)

This begins as a warning. No matter how godly we try to be, we must be aware of being led astray *"by the deceitfulness of sin."* How do we avoid this dangerous outcome? We *"encourage one another day after day."*

Before I go any further, now would be a good time to pause and examine your own life. Have you surrounded yourself with other believers who can encourage you, challenge you, and hold you accountable? Do you regularly meet with Christians who can expose your blind spots and stimulate you to *"love and good works"* (Hebrews 10:24)?

The kingdom of God is built on relationships. While it begins with our relationship with the Lord, He directs us into alignments, associations, and agreements with other people. He wants us to impact our culture, and our influence is maximized when we work together as a harmonious body and network of believers.

PROVOKE-A-THOUGHT:

"THE KINGDOM OF GOD IS BUILT ON RELATIONSHIPS, FIRST WITH GOD, THEN WITH ONE ANOTHER."

Relationships define our destinies, and our degree of influence is determined by the strength of those relationships. To have lasting authority and influence, we must begin with an intimate relationship with God, empowering us to serve others and impact our culture.

Learning from Blue Heeler Dogs

I have a pastor friend in Houston, Texas, who had Blue Heeler dogs when he was growing up. A Blue Heeler lives, eats, and breathes to do one thing: round up sheep or cattle. One of my friend's neighbors had five hundred head of cattle to round up but didn't have enough Blue Heelers. So some of the neighbors got together and said, "Hey, why don't we bring all our dogs together, have some coffee and fellowship, and help our neighbor."

They all went out the next morning knowing it was time to let their Blue Heelers to do what they ate, breathed, and lived to do. With great anticipation, they opened the dogs' cages and said, "Go Blue. Go Blue."

To their surprise, these Blue Heelers that ordinarily loved to round up cattle began to look at one another other instead. No matter how much their owners said, "Go Blue," the dogs just ran around growling, sniffing, and checking one another out. Until they had finished, they totally ignored their masters' voices. Finally, they quit inspecting one another and went out and brought the cattle in.

The moral of the story is that there's a lot of work to be done, and we can't do it all alone. As leaders, we need one another. We must learn to come together, move past our barriers, and work together for a cause greater than ourselves.

Reaching Every Sphere of Society

Whenever I speak to a group of pastors, I ask them how many people they are pastoring in their city. They might say fifty, five thousand, or twenty thousand; but then I ask, "Well, what's the population of your region?" For example, the Houston region has as many as six million people. That's a lot of people! This helps pastors see the magnitude of the task before them. They begin to understand that they're not just called to pastor a congregation; together with other leaders, they are called to co-pastor an entire region.

You see, when we grasp this truth, we realize that leadership is not a matter of building our own personal kingdoms. We need a much greater vision, encompassing the entire community and impacting every element of culture.

Perhaps you've heard about the church's mandate to impact the "seven mountains," or the "seven spheres" of our culture—business, government, media, arts and entertainment, education, family, and religion. These seven battleground areas of society were identified in 1975 by three notable change agents: Bill Bright, Loren Cunningham, and Francis Schaeffer.

The culture will be won or lost based on how we influence these seven spheres. Too many Christians think of ministry as something that occurs only within the walls of a church. Nothing could be further from the truth! Jesus said we're called to be the salt and light (see Matthew 5:13–16), and this applies to *every* area of life.

Notice what Paul told the believers in Corinth: *"Thanks be to God, who always leads us in triumph in Christ, and manifests through us the sweet aroma of the knowledge of Him in every place"* (2 Corinthians 2:14 NASB). You and I are supposed to be dispensers of the sweet fragrance of Jesus Christ—not just in church but *"in every place."* This means in your home and while you're at work or school. And you might even be called to infiltrate government, media, or arts and entertainment on behalf of the kingdom of God.

God has uniquely gifted each of us to impact the realm where He has placed us. We may be working at the supermarket or at a restaurant, or perhaps at a school or at the courthouse. We may even be called into the world of music or entertainment. But no matter where God sends us, our ultimate job is to be His ambassadors and representatives. (See 2 Corinthians 5:20.)

Sometimes, representatives of Christ have been referred to as "cultural evangelists" or "marketplace missionaries." As someone once observed, "Crossing the sea won't make you a missionary, but seeing the Cross will." No matter where we live or what kind of job we have, we are called to lift high the name of Jesus. Our true citizenship is in heaven (see Philippians 3:20), and God has commissioned us to bring heaven's resources and values to bear on our sphere of influence on earth.

Beyond the Church Walls

Too many churches are entirely wrapped up in what's happening within their four walls. They fail to empower people to be salt and light in every segment of society.

One of the most familiar phrases of the Great Commission is, "*Go into all the world and preach the gospel to all creation*" (Mark 16:15 NASB). Oral Roberts used to point out that this mandate is not just about world missions. Yes, it instructs Christians to take the gospel to other countries, but it also means taking the kingdom message to "everyone's world," or to every area of our society. *The Message* translation says, "*Go everywhere and announce the Message of God's good news to one and all*" (Mark 16:15 MSG).

Simply hiding out in our comfortable church meetings and withdrawing from society will never work. Changing these pillars of society will require courageous, persistent willingness of God's followers working together to confront the enemy. We'll never do it all alone, especially since each of us is called to a distinctly different mission field. To reach the whole world—everyone's world—we need the whole church. All hands on deck!

I like to think of this as the difference between using a fishing pole and a fishing net. If I use a fishing pole, I can catch only one fish at a time; but if I use a fishing net, I can catch a lot of fish. I have to become a part of something bigger—a net that has been knit together and spread upon the water. God calls us to be knit together and work toward a cause greater than ourselves. We're designed to function as part of a fishing net rather than an individual hook that can catch only one fish at a time.

There are two reasons why we need to grasp this principle of working together. As I just explained, it's the only way we can effectively fulfill the Great Commission. Furthermore, and this is a *personal* benefit here, we need to be linked hand in hand with other believers and other leaders in order to fulfill our own calling and finish the race well.

Impacting the Business Community

One of the great joys of my being in ministry over the years has been the privilege of being a friend to—and asked to help mentor—several Christian leaders who are powerfully impacting the business community. One of these leaders is Tan Sri Francis Yeoh, managing director of the YTL Group, based in Malaysia. Our friendship dates back over twenty-five years, when I met him while speaking at a businessmen's luncheon in Kuala Lumpur.

YTL is one of the largest companies on the Kuala Lumpur Stock Exchange, owning and managing regulated assets for more than ten million customers, assets that include utilities, high-speed rail, cement manufacturing, construction contracting, property development, hotels and resorts, and technology incubation. The company has won numerous awards, including being named as one of Asia's Best Companies in 2002.

Yeoh travels easily in and out of offices of heads of state, palaces of kings, and international summits on business and economics, yet he still takes time to reach out and share his resources with the needy. His philosophy can be summed up in a statement he made at a conference several years ago: "As a Christian, I see God as the Creator of the universe, and we are stewards of His wealth. God writes the script. We are His potentially powerful pencils."

God has granted Yeoh great favor, not only in his own country but around the world. He stewards his wealth and influence with compassion and sensitivity to those of all economic classes. He acknowledges publicly that Christ has the answer for our world's social ills, and he allows the Lord to use him as part of that answer.

Your Life Is Not Your Own

I love the popular worship song that says, "I give myself away…my life is not my own."[5] But these can't be mere words that we sing. They must be a reflection of who we are—not just in our worship services but all week long.

Hopefully the message has already come through loud and clear in this book: It's not about us; it's all about Jesus.

Saul of Tarsus learned this the hard way. On his way to Damascus to persecute Christians, he had a powerful encounter with the risen Christ. After Saul and his companions fell to the ground, he heard a voice from heaven say, "*Saul, Saul, why are you persecuting Me? It is hard for you to kick against the goads*" (Acts 26:14). In the passage below, notice that Saul received more than just a ticket to heaven that day. Jesus also gave him a new purpose in life.

> *Rise and stand on your feet; for I have appeared to you for this purpose, to make you a minister and a witness both of the things which you have seen and of the things which I will yet reveal to you. I will deliver you from the Jewish people, as well as from the Gentiles, to whom I now send you, to open their eyes, in order to turn them from darkness to light, and from the power of Satan to God, that they may receive forgiveness of sins and an inheritance among those who are sanctified by faith in Me.* (Acts 26:16–18)

You see, before this life-changing experience, Saul was a proud and headstrong man. But everything changed on the road to Damascus, just as *our* lives will change when we experience the power of the Cross and resurrection. When our lives are no longer our own, we can experience God's

---

5. William McDowell, "I Give Myself Away," 2009.

great purpose and plan in a whole new way. (See Jeremiah 29:11.) Instead of stubbornly kicking against the *"goads,"* we will find fantastic peace in the *"good and acceptable and perfect will of God"* (Romans 12:2).

I want to be clear on this: God wants to give you a purpose in life that is greater than yourself. Just like Saul—who later became known as the apostle Paul—your life will turn around when you encounter the crucified and resurrected Christ. He will then remove the scales from your eyes so you'll have a new revelation of the person He has called you to be.

Seeking First the Kingdom

I am quite grieved when I see Christian leadership materials that basically mimic the leadership principles of the world. You probably have seen them, too: "How *you* can have a bigger ministry, attract more people, raise more funds, and have a bigger platform." While there is nothing wrong with any of these objectives, too often they're pursued with the wrong motive.

You see, it's never supposed to be about *your* ministry or platform. It's about *His* kingdom! And Jesus made it clear that the principles of gospel leadership are far different from the principles of worldly leadership. (See Mark 10:42–45.) By promoting worldly lordship instead of biblical servanthood, some Christian preachers have blurred the lines, which has led to many shipwrecks among the people of God.

In contrast to the self-promotion and self-aggrandizement we see in some Christian leaders today, there are those who truly know they've been crucified with Christ. Leonard Ravenhill offered a vivid description of such a man—the apostle Paul, who…

> Had no ambitions—and so had nothing to be jealous about. He had no reputation—and so had nothing to fight about. He had no possessions—and therefore nothing to worry about. He had no "rights"—so therefore he could not suffer wrong. He was already broken—so no one could break him. He was "dead"—so none could kill him.[6]

---

6. Leonard Ravenhill, *Why Revival Tarries* (Bloomington, MN: Bethany House Publishers, 1959, 1987), 164.

One of the fundamentals of our faith is found in this statement by Jesus: *"Seek first the kingdom of God and His righteousness, and all these things shall be added to you"* (Matthew 6:33). Notice that Jesus said nothing at all about your kingdom or mine—it's all about His kingship and extending His reign over every area of our lives.

Sometimes, people worry that if they're truly sold out for God's kingdom, they will end up lacking the basic necessities of life. But look at what Jesus promises here: If we put the Lord's kingdom and righteousness first in our life, *everything else* will be added to us! Our heavenly Father loves us and promises to meet every need when we put Him first. (See Philippians 4:19.) That's good news, isn't it?

PROVOKE-A-THOUGHT:

"OUR RELATIONSHIPS GIVE DEFINITION
TO OUR DESTINIES. THE DEGREE OF INFLUENCE
WE HAVE IS DETERMINED BY
THE LEVEL OF THOSE RELATIONSHIPS."

7

Words of Affirmation and Trust

Marlene Yeo is the director of Somebody Cares New England, and she's having an incredible impact throughout her region. She has favor with everyone, from government officials and church leaders to gang members and homeless people. God is really blessing her, and it's wonderful that she's connected to our ministry.

My association with Marlene began years ago when we both attended an event in New York City. A mutual friend set up a meeting for us in a restaurant, and for several hours Marlene just wept and wept as she shared her heart for the needy and I explained the vision of Somebody Cares.

Years later, Marlene wrote a book about her ministry, and she described this encounter as a pivotal time in her life. Concerning her uncontrollable tears, she had thought at the time, "Doug probably was wondering what's wrong with this lady!" But then she explained why the meeting was so emotional for her: "Doug was giving me language to something I didn't know how to communicate."

I have to chuckle when I look back on this. I didn't really do much to help Marlene that day. The vision was already in her, and all I did was provide the language to communicate it, and affirm what God had already given her. Today she's doing great things for the kingdom of God, but I certainly can't take credit for any of it.

This is the kind of thing you and your fellow leaders should be doing for one another on a regular basis. We should be illuminating the giftings the Lord has put into one another's lives. When that happens, God's favor is unleashed and lives are touched. The Holy Spirit empowers us in ways that are far beyond our human capabilities.

You see, discouragement is one of the biggest obstacles to finishing well as a Christian leader. Each of us needs a regular dose of encouragement, first from the Lord, and then from other leaders and friends. In order to have any impact, it's crucial that we operate in faith—a reckless abandonment to believe and obey God. And obeying the Lord happens more readily when we learn how to encourage ourselves in the Lord (see 1 Samuel 30:6) and receive encouragement from others (see 1 Samuel 23:16).

A Lesson from My Childhood

Faith is a powerful thing. Jesus said that even faith the size of a mustard seed can move mountains (see Matthew 17:20), so it really doesn't take a whole lot of faith to do amazing things for God's kingdom. However, I've found that our faith is often undermined due to a problem in really trusting the Lord.

My biological father was an underwater demolition frogman during the Korean and Vietnam Wars. Today, these special forces have become known as the Navy Seals. One day he took me to the Naval Amphibious Base in Coronado, California, intending to teach me how to swim. He got me some authentic goggles and fins, just like the Navy Seals used. I was really pumped.

When we arrived, my dad jumped in the water and swam around for a while. He was a remarkable swimmer, so comfortable in the water that he looked like a fish. All of a sudden, he called out to me, saying, "Come on in, boy. Come on in."

At that moment, I stood frozen on the edge of the water. It was an issue of trust. Although I was confident my father was a great swimmer, I had to decide whether I trusted him to take care of *me* if I jumped into the water. I probably would have trusted him to catch me if he were sober, but he had been drinking.

I'm embarrassed to admit that I struggled to get into the water that day because I didn't trust my father. In fact, I've never really learned to properly tread water even to this day. I eventually taught myself to jump off a diving board and swim across the pool. But I struggle to tread water because of that frightening moment at the amphibious base when I felt a broken trust with my father.

Perhaps you're wondering what this story has to do with awakening your potential as a Christian leader. The answer is this: God will never give you a reason to distrust Him. You can safely jump into His loving arms, and He will never drop you or let you down. Jesus promised that no one can snatch you out of the Father's hands. (See John 10:27–29.) Scripture says, *"The eternal God is your refuge, and underneath are the everlasting arms"* (Deuteronomy 33:27).

My Stepfather's Criticism

When I was in high school, I loved to participate in sports. I went directly from football to wrestling to baseball, and I enjoyed playing all three. But although I had some success as an athlete, I sometimes ran into conflict with my stepfather. Let me explain.

My stepfather was a natural athlete, seemingly great at every sport. He was especially gifted at baseball, and he was one of the youngest men ever drafted to play on a farm club for a major league baseball team. However, before my stepfather could fulfill his dream of being a professional athlete, he got in trouble with the law. He and some buddies had stolen hubcaps and done other things that landed them in juvenile court.

Instead of changing his ways, my stepfather ended up lying about his age and joining the National Guard as a teen to stay out of jail. Then he transferred to the Navy, where he became a Navy Hospital Corpsman.

I'm sharing all of this background so you'll have a better understanding of the kind of men my father and stepfather were. My father and stepfather both loved and served this nation honorably, loved their families and made many sacrifices for the nation and their families. In fact, they both eventually died of military-related cancers. In retrospect, I have many good memories of the good times and of their investment in my life. Although they were great at what they did, my relationship with both of them was marred by their drinking.

One day, my stepfather was watching one of my baseball games. I was playing second base, and there was an opponent on first base. The ball was hit right to me, and I quickly caught it and touched second base. Then I threw it as hard as I could to first base, narrowly completing a double play. I was so excited! It's not every day that you get to make a double play. And I loved hearing my friends in the crowd scream my name and say, "Way to go, Dougie!"

However, in the midst of all this celebrating, I heard a loud voice in the crowd angrily cursing and criticizing my play. My stepdad had been drinking and he hadn't liked something about how I fielded the ball on the double play. Unbelievable—yet it really hurt.

On another occasion, I was playing on our school's varsity football team, and we had a party at our house after one of the games. It had been a rough game against one of the best teams. My stepdad refused to even talk with me, because he was that disappointed in how I had played. When I tried to shake his hand, he angrily slapped it away. I was so hurt by the incident that I slammed my fist into something, breaking my little finger.

Do you have any similar memories from your childhood? Were there times when you simply couldn't live up to the expectations of your father or mother or guardian, no matter how hard you tried? Or perhaps there were incidents later in life when you were unfairly criticized by your spouse, your children, or your boss.

Experiences like this—especially when authority figures are involved—can really warp our perspectives of both God and ourselves. Fortunately, our heavenly Father never treats us that way. As long as we've done our best, He's always proud of us. All He ever asks is that we yield to Him and make ourselves available.

The good news is that I ended up having a great relationship with both my father and my stepfather before they entered the portals of heaven. In fact, God allowed me to be a primary instrument in bringing them both to Christ. Although their lives were short in this world, I know they are rejoicing in heaven.

Reflecting Our Heavenly Father

I love the scene in the movie *Forrest Gump* in which Forrest's friend says, "Run, Forrest, run!" When I'm in the presence of my heavenly Father, I hear similar words of encouragement: "That's My boy! You can do this, Doug. Run, Doug, run!"

When we regularly take time to listen to that heavenly voice of encouragement, how can we fail? Even during times of adversity, we can shake off discouragement. Assured of our heavenly Father's love, acceptance, and affirmation, we can run the race and finish well.

We each hear *other* voices every step of the way. There are critics, naysayers, and backbiters. Amid all the chatter, noise, and distractions of life, we must set our hearts to hear our Father's voice above all others.

This is no small task. Our self-image and effectiveness as leaders are largely determined by what voices we listen to. Remember the prophet Elijah? One day he was boldly confronting hundreds of false prophets in the name of the Lord, and the next day he was terrified and depressed because he had made the mistake of listening to Queen Jezebel's threats! (See 1 Kings 18–19.)

Not only will your *own* life be affected by the voices you listen to, but you eventually will impart those messages—whether true of false—to the people you lead. We see this reflected in the Pharisees and Sadducees of Jesus' day. Since they didn't have a personal relationship with God as their heavenly Father, they developed twisted notions of what He was like.

PROVOKE-A-THOUGHT:

"DISCOURAGEMENT CAN KNOCK THE WIND OUT OF YOU AND BE A POWERFUL AND DEPRESSING DRUG. *'HOPE DEFERRED MAKES THE HEART SICK'* (PROVERBS 13:12). KEEP YOUR VISION OF HOPE. KEEP YOUR EYES ON THE LORD."

Soon, these religious leaders were utterly convinced that God was exactly like them: judgmental, legalistic, stingy, and slave-driving. The image they projected of Him was a faraway judge who was continually angry and impossible to please. In their mind, rather than ever being happy with His children, God was always on the lookout for reasons to punish people.

Sympathy for the Pharisees

As odd as it may sound, I feel sorry for these misguided religious leaders. Yes, the Pharisees were giving their followers a very warped view of the Father, but they had a somewhat valid excuse: They were simply passing on to others the inaccurate and unfortunate concept of God they had learned. Since they had never really experienced the love, grace, and mercy of the heavenly Father, they were unable to pass it on to others.

Do you see why our perception of God is so important? No matter what role of leadership we've been given, we will inevitably impart our view of God to others. No wonder Jesus imparted an entirely different view of God. Not only did He have a personal relationship with the heavenly Father, but He also said, *"He who has seen Me has seen the Father"* (John 14:9). His life was the perfect reflection and embodiment of the Father, *"the brightness of His glory and the express image of His person"* (Hebrews 1:3).

Instead of pointing our finger at the failings of the Pharisees and Sadducees, we need to examine our own view of God and assess how we reflect that image to those we lead. When people look at us, do they see an accurate representation of our heavenly Father? Can they see the honesty, kindness, and compassion of Jesus in our lives? Our mission on earth is to know God and make Him known, and we want to make Him known as He *really* is.

I want people to see the characteristics of Christ in me. I don't want my epitaph to say, "He was busy for his God," but rather, "He knew and reflected his God." Through my encouraging words, prayers, acts of kindness, handshakes, or smiles, I want to point people to Jesus as the Answer to all their needs. (See Matthew 5:16.)

Restoring Lost Trust

Based on the promises of Scripture, we should be able to put absolute trust in our heavenly Father. However, today we have a whole generation of people who struggle to comprehend the love of their heavenly Father, because they've never experienced a trusting relationship with an earthly father. Even those of us who have had good relationships with our earthly parents have been impacted on some level by the fatherless culture that now surrounds us.

As I think about my own life, I know I was negatively affected by my lack of trust in my biological father and my stepfather. Thankfully, God has revealed Himself to me—in the Bible and through my personal relationship with Him—as a good, good Father.

What about you? Have you experienced relationships in the past that caused you to lose trust? Perhaps your parents, your spouse, your boss, your pastor, or some other person let you down or betrayed your confidence in them. Maybe you've experienced the trauma of a broken home or a church split. Inevitably, such experiences take a toll on our level of trust.

So how can we effectively lead others to greater faith if we don't trust God ourselves? I encourage you to reflect on your life today, asking the Holy Spirit to show you areas where you've experienced broken trust. Ask Him to bring you hope and healing, restoring your ability to put your full trust in Him. And as part of the healing process, take time to meditate on the promises in Scripture that describe God's love and faithfulness.

Knowing Our Father's Voice

While working on the executive committee of a prayer movement in Philadelphia years ago, I met a man who was retired from Wall Street. Even though he had had a busy and stressful career, he had made sure that he never missed his kids' sporting events or other activities.

One of his sons became a highly recruited athlete, and before one of his games, his father apologetically said to him, "Son, I'm really proud of you, and I love coming to your events. I know I get a little crazy in the stands cheering for you. So if it embarrasses you to have me come and cheer so wildly, please let me know."

The son quickly replied, "Dad, don't you see? It's not like that at all. Even though there are thousands of people out there cheering and screaming, I hear only your voice amid all the noise."

When the man told me this story, I was really hit by the son's statement. Do you see how this could change our lives as leaders if we applied it to our relationship with our heavenly Father? What if, in the midst of so much noise, external pressures, and worldly distractions, we could shut it all out, hearing only the voice of God? Think of how our lives would change!

You see, everyone who has ever lived, young or old, is basically looking for three things: affirmation, acceptance, and approval. We especially long to hear our parents' affirming words "That's my boy," or "That's my girl." Yet many young people today are growing up without this kind of affirmation; many are being raised in broken homes.

It's hard to understand the love of a heavenly Father if you haven't experienced love and acceptance from your earthly parents. Even after I became a born-again Christian, it took me a while to understand the great love my heavenly Father had for me.

If you never receive much affirmation, acceptance, and approval from your earthly parents, the Bible still offers you good news about the kind of life and leadership you can experience. But the transformation is dependent on an ever-deepening relationship with Father God.

In His message to the multitudes, Jesus said,

> *What man is there among you who, if his son asks for bread, will give him a stone? Or if he asks for a fish, will he give him a serpent? If you then, being evil, know how to give good gifts to your children, how much more will your Father who is in heaven give good things to those who ask Him!* (Matthew 7:9–11)

Jesus is saying that even if a person has a loving and kind earthly father, the love of the heavenly Father is far, far better. He delights in giving "*good things to those who ask Him.*"

The apostle Paul described us as children adopted into the family of God. (See Ephesians 1:5.) We've been given a new position in Christ, "by which He made us accepted in the Beloved" (Ephesians 1:6). Our Father "has qualified us to be partakers of the inheritance of the saints in the light" and has placed us in "the kingdom of the Son of His love" (Colossians 1:12–13). If you truly grasp this, you'll never lack affirmation, acceptance, or approval again. That should be very exciting news!

I have a painting of Jesus being baptized by John the Baptist in the Jordan River. When the Lord came up from the water, He heard the Father's voice from heaven: "This is My beloved Son, in whom I am well pleased" (Matthew 3:17). The Message translates this, "This is my Son, chosen and marked by my love, delight of my life." The Father was saying, in effect, "That's My Boy! And I'm so proud of Him!"

When you are abiding in Christ, you can be assured that your heavenly Father has this very same love for you. Maybe you never received the love and affirmation you desired from your earthly parents. Perhaps they were too busy, stressed out, or constantly angry. Maybe they were addicted to alcohol, drugs, or the pursuit of success in their career.

Whatever your situation, today you can learn to trust again. As you step out in faith, trusting your heavenly Father's promises, you will find Him faithful—and your faith will grow.

PROVOKE-A-THOUGHT:

"FOSTERING AND FOCUSING ON OUR DISAPPOINTMENTS CAN LEAD TO DISILLUSIONMENTS THAT DISTRACT US FROM A GREATER DESTINATION. REMEMBER, GOD'S LOVE NEVER DISAPPOINTS."

8

The Value of Mentors—
and Critics

Courageous, transformational leadership must be rooted in the values of God's kingdom. Dr. Edwin Louis Cole once said, "The characteristics of the kingdom emanate from the characteristics of the King." You see, above all else, we're called to reflect the nature of Jesus Christ, our Savior and King. Society will not be impacted by persuasive arguments unless they are presented by people who model genuine Christlikeness, and this is even more important if we are leaders.

What traits did Jesus demonstrate to His disciples? While many leaders throughout the centuries have reached for thrones to build their own kingdoms, Jesus reached for a towel to wash people's feet. (See John 13:1–17.) That same heart of humility and servanthood is what it will take today to bring long-term transformation to the seven key areas of our culture.

The Bible says you are called to be an ambassador of God's kingdom. (See 2 Corinthians 5:20.) Whether you're a good ambassador or a bad one, your example will make an impression on people; and when you accurately reflect kingdom values, you will leave a lasting legacy, changing individuals and institutions for the glory of God.

But make no mistake, the core values of God's kingdom and His Word are under fierce assault today. The Bible describes timeless and nonnegotiable principles and values, but we live in an increasingly secular and relativistic culture. It has become fashionable to discard absolutes in favor of a mind-set reminiscent of Israel in the days of the judges: *"In those days there was no king in Israel; everyone did what was right in his own eyes"* (Judges 21:25).

So how are God's people supposed to live in times like these? First, we must recognize what is happening in the culture around us. As an old Bob Dylan song once declared, "The Times They Are A-Changin'." And the changes are not minor in nature—they are *foundational.*

King David asked a profound question of how we should live in days like these: *"If the foundations [of a godly society] are destroyed, what can the righteous do?"* (Psalm 11:3 AMP). First, we must ensure that our own spiritual foundation is strong. Like the wise man who built his house on rock instead of sand, we must listen to God's instructions and obey them. (See Matthew 7:24–27.)

> **PROVOKE-A-THOUGHT:**
>
> **"THE CHARACTER OF ANY KINGDOM (OR NATION) EMANATES FROM THE CHARACTER OF ITS KING (LEADER). WE MUST HAVE THE CHARACTER OF OUR KING TO WALK IN HIS INFLUENCE AND HIS AUTHORITY."**

Mentors in Perilous Times

We shouldn't be surprised by the times that are now upon us. The Bible clearly warns us about the *"perilous times"* that will come in the last days:

> *Men will be lovers of themselves, lovers of money, boasters, proud, blasphemers, disobedient to parents, unthankful, unholy, unloving, unforgiving, slanderers, without self-control, brutal, despisers of good, traitors, headstrong, haughty, lovers of pleasure rather than lovers of God,*

having a form of godliness but denying its power. And from such people turn away! (2 Timothy 3:1–5)

Paul wrote these words to his spiritual son Timothy. After warning him not to be swayed by the godless culture around him, Paul commended Timothy for following his *"doctrine, manner of life, purpose, faith, longsuffering, love, perseverance, persecutions, afflictions..."* (2 Timothy 3:10–11). In other words, the antidote to following people's bad examples is to find godly mentors like Paul and follow their Christlike examples.

What about you? Do you have a positive role model and mentor in your life? Someone who both encourages you and holds you accountable? A person who can boldly say, *"Follow my example, as I follow the example of Christ"* (1 Corinthians 11:1 NIV)?

God has graciously blessed me with some outstanding mentors, and I am eternally grateful for the rich deposits they've made in my spiritual life as a Christian leader. But today, as in Bible times, spiritual fathers and mothers are rare.

Look at how Paul described his fatherly love for the believers in Corinth:

I do not write these things to shame you, but to admonish you as my beloved children. For if you were to have countless tutors in Christ, yet you would not have many fathers, for in Christ Jesus I became your father through the gospel. Therefore I exhort you, be imitators of me.
(1 Corinthians 4:14–16 NASB)

Paul made it clear to the Thessalonians that being a spiritual father or mother is entirely different than being just a good preacher or Bible teacher:

Having so fond an affection for you, we were well-pleased to impart to you not only the gospel of God but also our own lives, because you had become very dear to us. (1 Thessalonians 2:8 NASB)

You see, it's all about relationship. Paul had genuine affection for people. He didn't just preach to them; he also gave them *his life.*

If you don't presently have such a person in your life, I encourage you to make this a matter of urgent prayer. Having a mentor to train and equip you will be a huge safeguard as you continue your quest to bear more fruit for God's kingdom, and he or she will help you finish well in the course He has set before you.

Dealing with Critics

Just as mentors can be a tremendous blessing and inspiration in our lives, critics and naysayers can bring us great discouragement if we let them. But it's impossible to go through this life without having any critics. Rather than alarm us, this should actually encourage us! Jesus told us plainly,

> *Blessed are you when they revile and persecute you, and say all kinds of evil against you falsely for My sake. Rejoice and be exceedingly glad, for great is your reward in heaven, for so they persecuted the prophets who were before you.* (Matthew 5:11–12)

The good news is that if God is for us, we have nothing to fear from those who oppose us. (See Romans 8:31.) However, the world takes note of how we behave when we're criticized or under attack. When we're treated harshly and unfairly, they look to see whether we manifest the character of Christ or respond according to the flesh.

Of course, there's something much more important than whether people are impressed by how we react to hardships. I've learned that how I respond during adversity often determines whether God's blessings in my life are expedited or postponed. Whenever I start to complain about some trial I'm going through, the Lord tells me, "Doug, remember that your attitudes and responses have consequences." Over the years, I've seen that every adversity is an opportunity for God to show Himself greater.

I've also learned that my *adversaries* often become my *advocates* when I keep a right spirit. I remember a time when I was transitioning out of the fitness business because God was leading me to establish a Christian activity center. I had great passion for what God had done in my life, and many people were coming to the Lord.

However, not everyone was thrilled by the direction God was taking me, especially since the transition was coming at great personal sacrifice. I had given away my car to Teen Challenge, a drug rehab ministry. And after ministering to a woman on the verge of suicide, I ended up giving her my furniture. So, with few earthly possessions left, I was basically living out of my suitcase at my fitness studio.

One day, a young pastor pulled up in his new, expensive sports car and disdainfully told me, "Those who are *really* in God's will are blessed with abundance."

As his car screeched off, I found myself very grieved. "Lord, is it true that I'm not being blessed?" I asked.

Later, the pastor called me and continued his barrage of criticism. "God is never going to use this crazy idea of yours," he said. "In the Bible, you never see the apostle Paul starting Christian activity centers or anything like that."

I tried to explain to this young man that I was just trying to reach people for Christ, but he continued to criticize me and for some time he remained an outspoken critic of mine. God used that experience to teach me a huge lesson that I've tried to live by all these years: Instead of harboring an offense against my adversaries and critics, I must bless and pray for them.

So I found the grace to pray for that young pastor, saying, "God, I pray that You'll do whatever it takes to open his eyes and see Your purposes here. In the meantime, help me to be what You want me to be, and help me to see any truth in what he is saying."

In the case of this brash pastor ridiculing my austere lifestyle, there was not a

PROVOKE-A-THOUGHT:

"CRITICS AND CRITICISM WILL COME AND GO, BUT CHRISTLIKE CHARACTER WITH COMMITMENT, CONSISTENCY, AND COURAGE WILL OUTLAST THEM ALL."

happy ending. He ended up committing adultery and lost his ministry as a result. He was so desperate that he called one day to ask if I could give him some preaching engagements. At first my flesh wanted to say, "Who do you think you are? You're getting exactly what you deserve." But I was challenged to humble myself. "What you need is not preaching engagements," I told him, "but I'll be happy to meet with you so we can pray together." Today I'm not exactly sure where this man is, but I've never stopped praying for God to restore him and use him.

The good news is, the Lord doesn't hold us responsible for how other people treat us or how they respond to our advice. But He *does* hold us responsible for how we respond to them. Are you dealing with critics in your life? If so, I hope you'll remember that every life experience can serve as a life lesson and become part of your life message, so don't let your trials go to waste!

Overcoming Evil with Good

When God teaches you an important lesson, it is seldom for you alone. He will almost always give you opportunities to share what you've learned with others.

> **PROVOKE-A-THOUGHT:**
>
> "DISCOURAGEMENT AND DISAPPOINTMENT BRING DISILLUSIONMENT, WHICH THEN BREEDS COMPROMISE AND DISTRACTS US FROM OUR INTENDED DESTINATION OR OUR DESTINIES."

After the Lord showed me how to deal with critics, I've been able to help and encourage other leaders who have faced similar situations. One of these leaders was Shaun, a friend in Australia who was connected with my ministry. Our parent organization had ordained him as a missionary and he had returned to his native country. He and his wife had started a small Bible study that grew into a multiethnic group of several hundred.

One day when I was visiting him, he told me how the pastor of one of the largest churches in his city was publicly railing against him and his small congregation. My friend was pretty distraught, as you might imagine, and he was initially skeptical of the advice I gave him.

"You need to take the high road," I said. "This defining moment will either limit or expand the future of your ministry. In fact, in addition to forgiving him, you need to start praying blessings over him. Let God vindicate you."

"Doug, you don't get this," he replied. "This man has a lot of influence, and he is speaking against me to anyone who will listen. He's undermining both me and my ministry."

At that point, I shared with my friend a powerful principle that I learned in David Wilkerson's book *Have You Felt Like Giving Up Lately?* Wilkerson pointed out that it's always the wrong person on the Cross. For example, Jesus was completely innocent and without sin, yet He was the One who had to bear the sins of others. Wilkerson also noted that if we hold on to the sins of other people, we will in essence hang on the Cross, feeling miserable, bitter, and wounded, while the other people go about their business. But if we make a decision to release and forgive those who say or do things against us, we are set free, once again able to fulfill God's purposes for our lives.

We all have faced injustice or unfair criticism at some point on our journeys, so we all must learn this vital lesson. Look at what the apostle Paul says concerning this:

> *Do not repay anyone evil for evil. Be careful to do what is right in the eyes of everyone. If it is possible, as far as it depends on you, live at peace with everyone. Do not take revenge, my dear friends, but leave room for God's wrath, for it is written: "It is mine to avenge; I will repay," says the Lord. On the contrary: "If your enemy is hungry, feed him; if he is thirsty, give him something to drink. In doing this, you will heap burning coals on his head." Do not be overcome by evil, but overcome evil with good.* (Romans 12:17–21 NIV)

As you allow these verses to sink in, I encourage you to pause for a moment to allow the Lord to search your heart. Is there someone you need to forgive and release? Are you willing to allow the Lord to be your Avenger and Healer, even if you have been deeply hurt? Even in your pain, will you reach out to them in love and kindness and bless them in any way you can?

Taking the High Road

My friend Shaun had a chance to act upon these verses in very practical ways. While I was still visiting him, he received some startling news: Serious sins had been discovered in the life of the pastor who had been so critical. He was publicly humiliated and had to step down from leadership in his church.

At first, my friend was tempted to gloat. "Well, see what I'm talking about, Doug?" he told me. "He's finally getting what he deserves."

"Oh, no, no, no!" I responded. "Remember, we were just talking about taking the high road." I encouraged him to reach out and give the man a call to find out if he was genuinely broken.

"Doug," he protested. "Don't you realize what he has done to me? And on top of that, he hates me, and there's no way he'll listen to anything I say."

"Take the high road," I insisted. "Reach out to him. You're not responsible for how he responds but how you respond."

Although he was mad at me for giving him such difficult advice, he later reached out to the pastor and called him. Rather than reject this overture, the pastor was so moved that he and his family sat under my friend's ministry for two years. He was ultimately restored to ministry and went on to pastor another church.

PROVOKE-A-THOUGHT:

"ALLOWING THE OFFENSES OF OTHERS TO KEEP US WOUNDED CAN HINDER US FROM ACCOMPLISHING GOD'S INTENDED PURPOSE AND DESTINY IN OUR LIVES."

Meanwhile, God blessed Shaun in amazing ways. At the time of my visit, he had several hundred members, but now his congregation numbers around three thousand. It's one of the largest churches in the area, and he also oversees an entire denomination that spans Australia and Asia.

I'm convinced that the outcome would have been much different if Shaun had chosen to hold on to his offense. That pastor probably wouldn't have been restored to ministry, and Shaun's church would never have grown past two or three hundred people. Thank God he took the high road!

9

A Foundation of Prayer

Hebrews 2:3 warns us not to *"neglect so great a salvation."* In the same way, we must be careful not to neglect the fundamentals of our faith and the necessary ingredients for spiritual growth. Yes, the flesh will war against the Spirit and make this difficult, but we must devote ourselves to the foundational disciplines of prayer, worship, studying God's Word, sacrificial giving, and always putting God's kingdom above our own interests.

Do you want to be guaranteed success in leadership? Do you want to finish the race well? There's nothing more important than practicing these personal disciplines on a consistent basis.

In order to awaken our leadership potential and finish the race well, we must address our personal spiritual disciplines. This does not come easy, because our flesh always wars against the Spirit, as Paul described in Galatians 5:16–17:

> *I say then: Walk in the Spirit, and you shall not fulfill the lust of the flesh. For the flesh lusts against the Spirit, and the Spirit against the flesh; and these are contrary to one another, so that you do not do the things that you wish.*

This means you shouldn't be surprised if your flesh struggles to submit to this biblical discipline. When I was in the fitness business, we used to say, "No pain, no gain." Things aren't much different in the Christian life.

As Dietrich Bonhoeffer observed, "When all is said and done, the life of faith is nothing if not an unending struggle of the spirit with every available weapon against the flesh."[7]

Prayer

One of the most crucial areas of personal discipline you'll need as a leader is prayer. This is not just an option; it's a necessity. As Leonard Ravenhill so powerfully described, prayer must be a top priority for every Christian leader:

> No man is greater than his prayer life. The pastor who is not praying is playing; the people who are not praying are straying.... We have many organizers, but few agonizers; many players and payers, few pray-ers; many singers, few clingers; lots of pastors, few wrestlers; many fears, few tears; much fashion, little passion; many interferers, few intercessors; many writers, but few fighters. Failing here, we fail everywhere.[8]

A consistent prayer life will never happen automatically or by a casual commitment. Your flesh will resist entering into a place of deep communication with God. But once you are there, you'll be very glad you made the choice.

Prayer is not meant to be complicated or super cerebral. It's simply communication with God. When practiced on a consistent basis, it produces intimacy with Him. As Dr. Edwin Louis Cole used to say, "Prayer produces intimacy to whom you pray, with whom you pray in agreement, and then for whom you pray." There's power when we go to God in prayer, and our prayers transcend geographic location, because the Lord is everywhere.

Developing a Pattern

Everyone has his own pattern when it comes to a life of prayer. My personal conviction is that I should never leave my house, hotel room, or

---

7. Bonhoeffer, *The Cost of Discipleship*, 171.
8. Ravenhill, *Why Revival Tarries*, 25.

wherever I am staying without praying twice each morning. This has become such a vital part of my life that I carry it out even when I've been pushing the snooze button on my alarm and wake up late. I'd rather not miss my morning moment with God, even if that means arriving late somewhere. These two morning prayer times aren't always as long as I'd like, but they are necessary in allowing God to put things in order as I begin my day.

My first prayer is what I call my horizontal time. It's the very first thing I do when I wake up. Before attempting anything else, I just lie down and begin to thank my heavenly Father for His love and goodness. "Father, I thank You," I typically say. "I'm not asking You for anything, but I just want to thank and praise You."

Then I go on to share various things I'm grateful for: "Father, thank You for this day You have made. Help me to rejoice and be glad in it. Father. I thank You for my family and my friends. I thank You, Lord, that You blessed me with a wonderful wife and daughter and mother-in-law, and I thank You for my co-laborers in ministry around the country and throughout the world." I could give additional examples of what I give thanks for, but I think you get the picture.

This small discipline has had tremendous repercussions in my life. Many people in this generation have never had much of a relationship with their earthly father. Often they haven't had consistent spiritual parents, either. So nothing is more important or powerful than fixing our attention on our heavenly Father as we begin each day. Though there is no set pattern for how we should pray, I think Jesus set a beautiful example when He taught us how to pray. Notice how He starts the prayer:

Our Father in heaven, hallowed be Your name. Your kingdom come. Your will be done on earth as it is in heaven. Give us this day our daily bread. And forgive us our debts, as we forgive our debtors. And do not lead us into temptation, but deliver us from the evil one. For Yours is the kingdom and the power and the glory forever. Amen.
(Matthew 6:9–13)

Of course, many people start their prayer times by diving right in to supplications and prayer requests, laying out their plans for the day. But I think that all should come later. My first prayer time is strictly a time of gratitude and thanksgiving. I encourage you to try this in your own life. Don't ask Him for a thing as you begin your prayer time. Just thank Him, thank Him, thank Him. Thank Him for His salvation, His grace, His wisdom, and His favor. Tell Him how grateful you are for His healing power, His strength, His provision, His protection, and His peace. You'll be amazed by how this simple exercise can transform your attitude and give you a new outlook on your day. Thanksgiving and praise are keys to experiencing God's presence all day long.

> *Enter into His gates with thanksgiving, and into His courts with praise. Be thankful to Him, and bless His name.*   (Psalm 100:4)

After I'm done thanking the Father—without asking for anything—I get up, take my shower, have my devotion time, and then I do what I call "knee time." I find a spot in my closet or at my bed to fall to my knees and give my day to the Lord.

This second prayer time goes something like this: "Lord, I know that in my human frailty, I'm not the most equipped or most qualified to do what I do. You've called me to do things I can do only with Your help. But since You've put me in these roles, I'm relying on You to equip me and empower me to do what I need to do today. Lord, help me to faithfully walk in all Your purposes for my life."

I also typically ask God to give me a right spirit, a clean heart, and a sharp mind. Then I pray, "Lord, may You be glorified in all that I think, do, and say." Sometimes I even call to mind a specific Scripture passage, like Psalm 19:14: *"Let the words of my mouth and the meditation of my heart be acceptable in Your sight, O LORD, my strength and my Redeemer."*

I've found that even when I do not remember all the things I prayed as I started my day, God always takes me at my word. Yes, I have frailties and flaws, and I make plenty of mistakes along the way, but I know the Lord hears my prayers, and He holds me to the commitments I've made to Him.

More than anything else, our heavenly Father just wants us to come into a place of communication and intimacy with Him. He wants our time with Him to consist of dialogues, not just monologues. Yes, He hears what is on our hearts, but He also wants to communicate what is on *His* heart.

I don't want you to think I always have hours to spend with the Lord in the morning. Sometimes, I have only a few moments because I'm late and rushing out the door for a meeting or appointment. But even if the time is brief, I always must have my horizontal prayer time of thanksgiving to the Father, followed by "knee time" to lay out my day before Him. Why are these prayer times so essential for me? Because I know I can't face my day without the Lord's favor upon my life.

Motivation and Consistency

When I speak about the importance of prayer at churches, conferences, and seminars, nearly everyone nods in agreement. In fact, I've hardly ever met a Christian who doesn't acknowledge that prayer is a powerful force. We all seem to know we should be more devoted to personal prayer and intercession, but we often lack the needed discipline to have a consistent prayer life.

In his essay "The Common Denominator of Success," Albert E. N. Gray wrote,

> The successful person has the habit of doing the things failures don't like to do. They don't like doing them either necessarily, but their disliking is subordinated to the strength of their purpose.

Notice the word *habit*. It's not enough to sporadically shoot a prayer up to God during a time of crisis. Prayer—and other spiritual disciplines like reading the Bible—needs to be a daily habit. As former Ohio State football coach Jim Tressel observed, "The hallmark of excellence, the test of greatness, is consistency."[9]

John Maxwell wrote in his book *The 15 Invaluable Laws of Growth*,

> When I started my speaking career, I believed that motivating people was the key to helping them succeed. *If I can get them moving in the right direction,* I thought, *they will be successful.*[10]

---

9. Jim Tressel, *The Winners Manual: For the Game of Life* (Carol Stream, IL: Tyndale House Publishers, Inc., 2008), 100.
10. John C. Maxwell, *The 15 Invaluable Laws of Growth: Live Them and Reach Your Potential* (Nashville, TN: Center Street, 2012).

You see, Maxwell is a well-known motivational speaker, and he recognizes that motivation is critically important to us all. "My goal was to inspire people so much that they'd be ready to charge hell with a water pistol," he recalls. "When I was done, I'd walk away thinking I'd done a good job. But often whatever motivation people received didn't seem to last very long."[11]

Over years of motivating people to make positive changes in their lives, Maxwell concluded that something was missing—an indispensable ingredient for lasting success:

> I'm still a big believer in motivation. Everyone wants to be encouraged. Everyone enjoys being inspired. But here's the truth when it comes to personal growth: Motivation gets you going, but discipline keeps you growing. That's the Law of Consistency. It doesn't matter how talented you are. It doesn't matter how many opportunities you receive. If you want to grow, consistency is key.[12]

Perhaps you've discovered this same principle at work in your own life or the lives of those you lead. You were motivated for a while, but you still weren't able to maintain your objectives or keep your resolutions.

If you struggle with discipline and follow-through, take a moment right now to ask the Lord to help you. Repent of any laziness, procrastination, excuses, or other factors that have diverted you from your objectives. Make a new commitment to turn your good intentions into lifelong habits.

The Place of Power

Although a consistent prayer life is indispensable to lasting success as a Christian leader, it's only the beginning. Our personal prayers can be supercharged when we come into agreement with our spouse and other believers.

> *If two of you agree on earth concerning anything that they ask, it will be done for them by My Father in heaven. For where two or three are*

---

11. Ibid.
12. Ibid.

gathered together in My name, I am there in the midst of them.
(Matthew 18:19–20)

This means that though our individual prayers are powerful, there's exponentially more power available to us when we unite in prayer with others. The Greek word translated *"agree"* here is *symphōnéō*, from which we get the English word "symphony."[13] It's a beautiful picture of the kind of harmony God wants His people to have as they pray together and work together in His kingdom.

This is seen throughout the Scriptures. The Holy Spirit was poured out on the day of Pentecost when the believers *"were all with one accord in one place"* (Acts 2:1). And we're told, *"How good and pleasant it is when God's people live together in unity! ...For there the LORD bestows his blessing"* (Psalm 133:1, 3 NIV).

So remember, private prayer is the key to public power, unleashing heaven's resources on the earth (see Matthew 6:10); and our power increases exponentially when we pray in unity with other believers and other leaders!

---

13. *symphōnéō*, HELPS Word-studies, http://biblehub.com/greek/4856.htm.

10

Transformed by
Authentic Worship

J ust as I've found it necessary to be intentional about my prayer life, I also must devote myself to regularly worshiping the Lord and entering into His presence. When some believers think of worship, they think of the pleasant feelings they get when they listen to contemporary Christian music. But true worship is not about goose bumps; it's about *transformation.*

> *We all, with unveiled face, beholding as in a mirror the glory of the Lord, are being transformed into the same image from glory to glory, just as by the Spirit of the Lord.* (2 Corinthians 3:18)

Can you imagine how Isaiah would respond if you asked him about the warm feelings he felt when worshiping in the presence of the Lord? Confronted with the holiness of almighty God, he cried out in agony,

> *Woe is me, for I am undone! Because I am a man of unclean lips, and I dwell in the midst of a people of unclean lips; for my eyes have seen the King, the* LORD *of hosts.* (Isaiah 6:5)

Instead of warm feelings or goose bumps, he experienced the searing pain of a burning coal touched to his lips as God purged him of iniquity and sin. (See Isaiah 6:6–7.) Once Isaiah had been cleansed and transformed in

God's awesome presence, he was finally ready to report for service: *"Here am I!"* he said. *"Send me"* (Isaiah 6:8).

The Heart of Worship

Believers today are under fierce attacks of the enemy in every area of life. Often, our only path to breakthrough is to invite God's presence through authentic, passionate worship. If you doubt me on this, take a look at King Jehoshaphat's amazing victory when surrounded by enemy armies. (See 2 Chronicles 20:1–30.) As the worshipers went out in front of the army and began to sing praise, the Lord set ambushes against their enemies!

Worship is such a powerful spiritual force, but I've found that it is often misunderstood. We tend to make it a matter of music, instruments, and our favorite praise bands. But all the while, true worship is a matter of the heart—and it's all about the Lord, not about us. This is beautifully expressed in Matt Redman's song "The Heart of Worship," in which he declares that a mere song is not what God requires of us when we worship. God looks for something much more authentic and from the heart. As Redman says, "I'm sorry, Lord, for the thing I've made it, when it's all about You; it's all about You, Jesus."[14]

It's interesting that the first time the word *worship* was used in Scripture it had nothing at all to do with music, instruments, or singing. Instead, it was used to describe Abraham's simple obedience in sacrificing his son Isaac on the altar. (See Genesis 22:5.) So, remember, authentic worship is all about giving God adoration and praise—and this is supposed to include doing *everything* in our life to glorify Him. (See 1 Corinthians 10:31.)

True worshipers recognize that even their best attempts to honor the Lord fall far short. This prayer from A. W. Tozer illustrates why we all need more hunger for the presence of God:

O God, I have tasted Thy goodness, and it has both satisfied me and made me thirsty for more. I am painfully conscious of my need

---

14. Matt Redman, "The Heart of Worship," Birdwing Music, Thank You Music, LTD., 1998.

of further grace. I am ashamed of my lack of desire. O God, the Triune God, I want to want Thee; I long to be filled with longing; I thirst to be made more thirsty still. Show me Thy glory, I pray Thee, that so I may know Thee indeed. Begin in mercy a new work of love within me. Say to my soul, "Rise up, my love, my fair one, and come away." Then give me grace to rise and follow Thee up from this misty lowland where I have wandered so long. In Jesus' name. Amen.[15]

I encourage you to pray these stirring words, asking the Lord to draw you into greater intimacy with Him.

An Antidote to Discouragement

There was a time in my life I was doing a lot of street ministry, often staying up until two, three, or four o'clock in the morning. I was working with runaways, drug addicts, and prostitutes in Lower Westheimer, one of the highest crime districts in the state of Texas.

One night I came home to my small apartment after a particularly rough night on the streets. People had been singing vulgar, degrading songs, and a man dressed like satan had run around punching people. It seemed that those of us trying to lift up the name of Jesus had no impact at all.

I was incredibly discouraged. I looked around my sparsely furnished apartment and wondered if I was just wasting my time. I had a J. C. Penney's couch and a mattress but no bed. I had a little crate that I used for a table, and the books in my study were spread all over the floor, because I had no bookshelves to shelve them. It broke my heart that despite my great love for the people on the streets, often they disregarded my message. I found myself so overwhelmed, I couldn't even cry. My energy was gone, and it seemed like this "ministry thing" just wasn't working out for me. It appeared that the only solution was to go back into the business world, where at least I could make some money.

---

15. A. W. Tozer, *The Pursuit of God with Study Guide: The Human Thirst for the Divine with Study Guide* (Camp Hill, PA: Zur Limited, 1982, 1993).

I went into my dark bedroom and fell down on my knees in front of the mattress. As I lay there, virtually paralyzed, I heard the Lord speak deeply into my heart, "Give Me a drink."

Startled, I turned the lights on and opened my Bible to John chapter 4, where Jesus told the woman at the well, "*Give Me a drink*" (John 4:10). I began to read that story, but at first I didn't see how it applied at all to my situation.

"Lord, in this case, *I'm* the one who needs a drink," I told Him. "I have nothing at all to give *You.*"

Then I sensed the Holy Spirit say, "It's not what you feel that counts, Doug. True worship is coming into a place of simple obedience, becoming a living worshipper."

Although my heart didn't change instantly, I turned out the lights and, out of simple obedience, started walking around and saying repeatedly, "Praise the Lord! Hallelujah! Thank You, Jesus!" Even though I'm not much of a singer, I started making a joyful noise (see Psalm 98:4; 100:1) and singing worship songs to the Lord, including "Praise the Name of Jesus" and "In My Life, Lord, Be Glorified."

As I paced back and forth and magnified the Lord in my dark apartment, the hours went by incredibly fast. What started as simple obedience turned into something else. Instead of just going through the motions out of obedience, authentic thanksgiving and adoration began to flow from my spirit. Instead of feeling beaten down and discouraged, I sensed that I was worshiping among a heavenly host of angels that night!

Just a short time earlier, I had been grumbling about my meager furnishings, but now my whole perspective was of praise. "Lord, I thank You for giving me a roof over my head," I said. "Thank You I'm not homeless, or out on the streets, or strung out on drugs. And thank You for my nice J. C. Penney couch and for the mattress on my bedroom floor."

It was an amazing time with the Lord. Soon the light of dawn was breaking through my window—just as God's light had broken through my discouraged heart hours earlier. Everything changed, not because I felt like worshiping the Lord, but because I gave Him the adoration He's so worthy of.

In those few hours, God had done far more in my life than I could have done in weeks or months of trying to kick my spiritual funk. His presence brought me *"fullness of joy"* (Psalm 16:11) once again, and His Spirit had hovered over my dark and dismal thoughts to bring order and His amazing light. (See Genesis 1:1–3.)

Simple Obedience

In 1990, I was asked to speak at a Full Gospel Business Men's Fellowship International (FGBMFI) luncheon in Kuala Lumpur, Malaysia, the country's capital city. A very distinguished gentlemen approached me and said, "Doug, I felt something churning inside me when you were speaking, and I wondered if you would help disciple me."

PROVOKE-A-THOUGHT:

"OUT OF SOME OF OUR MOST CHALLENGING AND DIFFICULT OF CIRCUMSTANCES, OUT OF OUR MOMENTS OF PAIN, GOD CAN BRING FORTH SOME OF OUR GREATEST OF TESTIMONIES."

It turned out that this man held the title "Tan Sri," which is the highest title anyone can be given in his country. It's similar to being knighted in England, and it's a title that can only be given by the prime minister or king. This is the same man I mentioned in chapter six.

Informed of his impressive credentials, I felt rather inadequate to help him. "Why are you telling me all these things?" I asked. "I live on the other side of the world, in Houston, Texas."

The man was insistent. "Something tells me that you'll be my friend and that you're someone I can trust."

So we became friends that day, and it has been a great blessing for me to be considered his friend throughout the years. In December 2013, I was extremely honored to be invited to Malaysia to help officiate at the beautiful wedding of his eldest son, Jacob, and Jacob's then fiancée, Geraldine.

A couple years after we met, I was back in Kuala Lumpur to speak at a meeting with some of his directors at the corporate headquarters. While introducing me, he gave a short teaching and told them, "You know, the highest form of worship is simple obedience to God."

I immediately replied, "Wow! That's really good. Can I borrow that statement sometime?"

With a smile, my friend said, "My brother Doug. You've already used that statement. In fact, I read it in your book!"

"Oh, okay, great," I replied.

I had forgotten that one of my books says, "Simple obedience is the highest form of worship." It was gratifying that a man on the other side of the world was putting this important truth into practice and even teaching it to others.

Later he told me of a time when he was in church and the Lord asked him, "Why do you worship Me?" He quickly understood what the Spirit of God was saying to him. You see, as a wealthy, influential business leader, he often had people try to get something from him through flattery and sweet talk. So he wanted to surround himself with people who valued him for who he was, not for what they could get from him. In the same way, he saw how it grieved God's heart when people approached Him only to get something in return.

It dawned on this man that he wanted to know who his real friends were, people who were genuine and trustworthy. He recognized that God is the same way. The Lord is looking for true worship and obedience, not just endless petitions. Instead of approaching Him with a "gimme gimme" attitude, as if He's a genie in a lamp, He wants us to adore Him for who He is and give Him the glory due His name.

Our Great Inheritance

I'm convinced that the greatest breakthroughs in our lives don't come when we just try to "make something happen." Sometimes people talk about taking their inheritance by force, but I think that they miss an important point: We don't have to twist our heavenly Father's arm in order to receive His blessings! The inheritance already belongs to us, so we can go ahead and start *"giving thanks to the Father who has qualified us to be partakers of the inheritance of the saints in the light"* (Colossians 1:12).

I love the story Jack Hayford tells about the time he and his brother Jim received an inheritance when their mother passed away. He noted that the inheritance didn't come because they earned it or deserved it. They hadn't done anything special to merit the inheritance—it came just because they were related to their mother and carried the name "Hayford."

In the same way, we receive an inheritance because of our relationship with our heavenly Father. Furthermore, our initial salvation and subsequent blessings are not based on our good works or merit. (See Ephesians 2:8–9; Titus 3:4–7.) We receive these things not because we live a perfect life, but because we carry the name of Jesus.

In fact, Paul says that because we're positioned in Christ—the Son of God's love—we've been blessed with *"every spiritual blessing in the heavenly places"* (Ephesians 1:3). Furthermore, we've been given a stewardship to bless others as He has blessed us. (See Genesis 12:2.) We're called to use our spiritual inheritance to bring honor and glory to His name. This is beautifully illustrated in the commission Jesus gave us in Matthew 5:14–16:

> *You are the light of the world. A city that is set on a hill cannot be hidden. Nor do they light a lamp and put it under a basket, but on a lampstand, and it gives light to all who are in the house. Let your light so shine before men, that they may see your good works and glorify your Father in heaven.*

Through the great inheritance we've received, God has put His light in us to dispel the darkness, gloom, and despair. But that isn't the end of the story. He has called us to shine that light to those in need.

Notice that although we didn't receive our inheritance because of any good works, Jesus said our heavenly Father will be glorified when we reach out to others with love and good deeds. When people see tangible expressions of the love of Christ, they will be drawn toward a relationship with Him.

11

Becoming Aligned with God's Word

Jesus made it clear that we will have a firm spiritual foundation only to the degree that we hear His words and do them. (See Matthew 7:24–27.) This includes aligning ourselves both with the written Word of God and the voice of His Spirit.

To some people, the Bible is just a matter of historical information or theological precepts. Instead of grasping the power of God's Word to change their lives, they've turned it into a dry, lifeless, irrelevant religious textbook.

Leonard Ravenhill once observed, "There is a world of difference between knowing the Word of God and knowing the God of the Word." Some of today's religious leaders, rather than allowing the Scriptures to draw them into a deeper relationship with the Father, have found "proof texts" to explain away His power to do miracles in their lives today. With their twisted interpretations, they not only box God out of their own lives but also impart dead religiosity to their followers.

In contrast, Scripture describes the life-changing impact God's Word is meant to have on us:

The word of God is living and powerful, and sharper than any two-edged sword, piercing even to the division of soul and spirit, and of joints and marrow, and is a discerner of the thoughts and intents of the

heart. And there is no creature hidden from His sight, but all things are naked and open to the eyes of Him to whom we must give account.
(Hebrews 4:12–13)

God's Word is *"living and powerful,"* my friends. Rather than just a religious rule book, the Bible reveals the thoughts and intentions of our hearts. There is nowhere to hide from its searchlight, and one day we *"must give account"* to the Lord for how we've responded to its teachings.

Some people, of course, want to turn this into an empty, legalistic routine. They prescribe how many minutes or hours a day we should read our Bible, and it becomes just another item to cross off our to-do list. But, remember, the Christian life is never about legalism but about relationship and obedience.

Wash Away the Filth

One of the great benefits of reading the Word of God is that it washes away the filth we're exposed to on a daily basis. We live in a morally polluted world, which is more pervasive than ever before. We see advertisements on billboards as we drive down the street, just minding our own business. We're exposed to marketing agendas in the magazines we pass while checking out at Walmart or at our local grocery store. Each day, we see or hear countless TV, radio, and Internet ads designed to appeal to our lower nature. And through no fault of our own, our ears take in loads of subliminal noise and corrupt messages through the music we hear at fitness centers, malls, and restaurants we visit.

What's particularly scary about this is how unconscious we are of the world's influence. Our minds and hearts pick up all sorts of destructive images and sounds, even when we're unaware of it. The Bible warned about this happening centuries ago (see Proverbs 4:23), and today modern technology has brought about an exponential rise in this danger.

We're told in Romans 12:2, *"Do not be conformed to this world, but be transformed by the renewing of your mind."* So how can we renew our mind? The primary way is by reading and meditating on the Scriptures, allowing the Holy Spirit to show us where our thoughts and attitudes are misaligned with God's truth.

Jesus washing His disciples' feet was more than just a lesson in servant leadership. (See John 13:1–17.) It was also a beautiful reminder that we live in a dirty, dusty world, and some of the dirt and dust inevitably clings to us as we walk through life. So we must intentionally take time to "wash our feet" by spending time in His presence and reading His Word. (See Ephesians 5:25–26.)

However, just as with worship, there will come times when we don't feel like opening the Scriptures to receive *"our daily bread"* (Matthew 6:11; see Mathew 4:4). Though the devil and our flesh may fight us on this, we need to be intentional about reading God's Word on a regular basis. Sometimes, we'll have to do this strictly out of obedience and self-discipline; other times, it will be a *delight.*

If you need some word pictures to help you understand this principle, ask yourself these questions: How do you think you would smell if you took a bath or shower only every month or two? Or how much strength would you have if you took a few bites of food only every four to five days? In the same way, God's Word is an indispensable part of your cleansing and your nourishment.

My Initial Struggle

When I first became a believer, I didn't comprehend much of the Bible. People told me how important it was to study the Word, but it made no sense to me. Whenever I tried to read a passage, I ended up frustrated. "What's that all about?" I would complain.

Then, one day, something amazing happened when I was in a restaurant talking to a friend. To my shock, I found myself telling him what I had been reading in the Bible—even though I'd thought my comprehension of it was nil. What a pleasant surprise to discover that the seeds of God's truth were taking root after all. More and more, I found myself putting the Word into practice and sharing it with others.

Like me, there will be times when your flesh is tired, when studying the Bible will be the last thing you feel like doing. At those times, you would rather watch the news, a game show, or a sporting event. But remember that there's no better way to wash, cleanse, and renew your inner person than to soak in the waters of God's Word. Sometimes mere moments in God's Word can cleanse away many hours of pollution from my mind and soul.

At times in my life, I've read several chapters each day. At other times, just one verse pops out at me, and the Holy Spirit tells me to stop and ponder it. It may even be a verse I've read hundreds of times before, but suddenly God gives me a life-changing revelation about it that I've never seen before.

Trusting God

As the old hymn by John H. Sammis reminds us,

Trust and obey, for there's no other way,
To be happy in Jesus, but to trust and obey.[16]

And in order to consistently live a life of trust and obedience, we must saturate our life with the promises of God's Word. Make no mistake about it: Your trust in God will be tested! Some days you will feel like giving up on His calling in your life. Other times, you will be tempted to hoard your resources out of fear you won't have enough.

When I left the business world and stepped out to obey God's call to ministry, it was very rough at times. I often found myself crying out to the Lord, "If You're really calling me to leave everything behind to serve You, I don't want to beg, borrow, and solicit for donations. I'm willing to trust You, but I never want to grovel for resources."

I had seen some people promote their ministry with high-gloss photos of themselves and ministry brochures to solicit speaking gigs, but I didn't want to do that. I simply wanted to obey God and reach out to hurting people. I wanted to share the good news of Jesus with the homeless, runaways,

---

16. John H. Sammis, "Trust and Obey," 1887.

drug addicts, prostitutes, gang members, and people who were lost and broken in other ways, just as I used to be lost and broken.

As I continued to reach out to needy people, who usually had nothing to give me in terms of financial support, I experienced amazing provision: Although I never seemed to have enough, God supernaturally supplied all my needs when I gave what I had! Yes, there were many financial needs in the ministry and in my personal life; but there was no need for me to beg in search of donations, for God was my Source and my Provider.

I remember one time when our bills were much more than we could afford. We had about five hundred dollars in the checking account, which wasn't nearly enough to meet the need. So what could I do? I could freak out and make emergency phone calls to people, saying, "You gotta help me. Things are desperate here." But I wasn't going to do that. My heavenly Father hadn't called me to be a beggar.

Don't get me wrong. I realize that ministries have to raise money. I've spoken at numerous fund-raisers for other ministries, helping them to raise funds for orphanages, compassion centers, youth homes, buildings, facilities, and equipment to further their ability to fulfill their mission. But God was teaching me to rely solely on Him.

PROVOKE-A-THOUGHT:

"PEOPLE WILL MAKE TIME FOR WHAT IS IMPORTANT TO THEM. PEOPLE SEEM TO ALWAYS AFFORD WHAT THEY REALLY WANT."

So I prayed, "Lord, I need a miracle." Then I took the five hundred dollars left in our account and sowed it into other ministries. I knew it wasn't going to cover the several-thousand-dollars-worth of bills, but it would bless someone else. So instead of walking in fear, I chose to walk in faith. I sowed out of my own need, and God began to do miracles.

Tested Again

On another occasion, our ministry faced an enormous shortfall, needing about $250,000 within just ten days. Once again, my natural tendency was to get on the phone and call some people to request financial help. But again, I couldn't do that.

I try to do everything out of relationship. I don't have a problem in sharing my heart with my family members, friends, and colleagues. Yet I'm not into cold calling, groveling, or spending all my time fund-raising, when God has called me to spend my time ministering to hurting people.

But this wasn't an easy time for me. I had to trust God in deeper ways than ever before, and He was asking me to let go of my paltry assets and sacrificially meet the needs of others, despite my own needs.

A couple of days later, I got a phone call from someone I had helped twenty years earlier, when he had dropped out of college and ended up on the streets, homeless and on drugs. He had become a very successful businessman.

"Doug," this man said, "as you know, my wife and children have never seen me on drugs or alcohol, because you helped me all those years ago. The Lord told me in prayer this morning to send $100,000 to your ministry."

Wow! I was simply blown away. I had never seen anything like that. The Holy Spirit had spoken to him during his prayer time; he hadn't even known of our urgent need.

A few days after that, I received a call from a man who was vacationing with his children in Spain. His said he'd had a powerful encounter with God. "The Lord woke me up this morning and said I needed to send $100,000 to you personally," he told me, making it clear that this gift was for me and not for the ministry.

I was in big financial need in my personal life at that time, as well. I couldn't help but think about all the things I could do with $100,000, such as paying off my mortgage and other expenses. And here this man was, offering to wire $100,000 to my personal account from Spain!

I had specifically prayed for the Lord to take care of the ministry, and I was confident He wanted to grant this request. As I thought about the situation, I remembered the story of God speaking to Solomon in a dream, saying, *"Ask! What shall I give you?"* (1 Kings 3:5). The Lord was pleased that Solomon didn't ask for anything for himself, but rather asked for wisdom to properly govern the people.

So I said to the person on the phone, "You know, I've always told you not to give to me personally."

"But that was a long time ago," he insisted. "No, I want to bless you."

Refusing to back down, I said, "If God has told you to give $100,000, then give it to the ministry." So he sent the money to our ministry.

After I did that, one of my friends scolded me, "Stringer, what did you do? You need the money, and you should have taken his gift."

However, this decision was consistent with my value system. I've made it a core value, so that I'm never tempted by power, fame, or money. I realized that if didn't set those parameters up front, it would be easy for me to compromise—and I didn't want to compromise. I determined that it's always better to err for the sake of the kingdom rather than for the sake of self, because God always takes care of faithful stewards.

In the days following that important stand, the rest of the $250,000 came in! I didn't have to beg; neither did I have to twist anyone's arm. Many of the gifts were remarkable, such as the $25,000 sent in by a movie producer who had read one of my books.

Entering God's Economy

You see, God will take care of the people who obey Him and stick to the core values found in the Word. But this requires intentionality in how they spend their time, talent, and resources. This is a crucial part of entering into God's economy.

Furthermore, in God's kingdom, there's reciprocity and multiplication beyond what we could ever provide for ourselves. This reciprocity is never a matter of one plus one equals two. Instead, it's about multiplication and exponential growth. This is like sowing an apple seed, which produces an entire tree, not just a single apple. And if I sow a seed of wheat or corn, it will produce a stalk, not just a grain of wheat or an ear of corn. In due time, every seed we sow and nurture will come back as a harvest, much greater than the seed itself. (See Galatians 6:7–10.)

God desires to give us an overflowing life (see Psalm 23:5); but in order to unlock His heavenly storehouses, we must unconditionally surrender our lives and resources to Him. (See Malachi 3:8–12.)

PROVOKE-A-THOUGHT:

"THE MOST PRICELESS COMMODITIES ARE NOT FOUND IN EARTHLY TREASURES, BUT IN HOW WE STEWARD OUR TIME, FRIENDSHIPS, AND RELATIONSHIPS."

12

The Matter of Attitudes

Keeping a right attitude can be incredibly difficult, especially when we're criticized or even lied to. Nevertheless, a right attitude is an indispensable key to successfully fulfilling God's promises in our lives and ministries. If we don't get this right, we'll find ourselves going around the mountain over and over again, and eventually we'll likely find ourselves out in the desert.

Your attitudes affect everything else in your life. Even your alignments, agreements, and associations can be undercut if we allow unforgiveness, bitterness, complaining, or other bad attitudes to take root in our hearts. And, as Albert Einstein once observed, "Weakness of attitude becomes weakness of character."

Countless relationships among Christians are broken when one or both parties take offense and fail to maintain a right spirit. Friendships have been destroyed, families have been torn apart, and churches have been split all due to failure to walk in God's love and forgiveness. Don't allow *your* peace of mind and effectiveness as a leader to be sabotaged by bad attitudes!

If God has called you to leadership, He wants you to walk in the fullness of His authority and influence in your allotted sphere. Along with a right attitude, you will need a right perspective, keeping your eyes on your destination so you can lead others to a place of victory. And it's a lot easier to keep your attitudes right if you have a clear vision of hope for your future.

One of the most tragic stories in the Bible was of Esau, son of Isaac and brother of Jacob. His life unraveled for a number of reasons, including bad choices, bad attitudes, and wrong priorities:

> *Pursue peace with all people, and holiness, without which no one will see the Lord: looking carefully lest anyone fall short of the grace of God; lest any root of bitterness springing up cause trouble, and by this many become defiled; lest there be any fornicator or profane person like Esau, who for one morsel of food sold his birthright. For you know that afterward, when he wanted to inherit the blessing, he was rejected, for he found no place for repentance, though he sought it diligently with tears.* (Hebrews 12:14–17)

This brief passage reveals some of the major reasons many leaders fail to finish well.

+ Instead of pursuing peace and maintaining a right attitude, Esau allowed a *"root of bitterness"* to spring up in his life.

+ Instead of pursuing holiness, he became a *"fornicator"* and *"profane person."*

+ Instead of maintaining right priorities and valuing his calling, he *"for one morsel of food sold his birthright."*

I encourage you to read this passage one more time, allowing the Holy Spirit to reveal to you any attitudes, conduct, or priorities that needs adjusted in your life.

PROVOKE-A-THOUGHT:

"WE ARE LIMITED, OR LEVERAGED, BY OUR ATTITUDES AND PERSPECTIVES IN LIFE. KEEP THE RIGHT ATTITUDE, RIGHT SPIRIT, AND PROPER PERSPECTIVE. A WRONG PERSPECTIVE FUELS A WRONG ATTITUDE AND LESSENS OUR INFLUENCE OR LEVERAGE."

Attractive Attitudes

I have a friend who was the general manager of one of the most successful P. F. Chang's China Bistros in the country. He has quite a testimony, too. At one time, he was on the FBI's Most Wanted list, but God did a miracle and transformed his life. Since then, he has used kingdom principles to build successful leadership teams at his restaurants.

One day, we were talking about this, and I asked him, "What is it that makes your P. F. Chang's restaurants so successful? You certainly have great food, and I know that is important; but it seems your restaurants have something more than that."

"There are a number of factors, Doug," he replied. "Of course, the product and presentation must be good, and it's important to maintain a good atmosphere, making it a place where people feel comfortable. But even if we've succeeded in all those factors, we'll lose customers if our service and team members' attitudes are bad. No marketing budget in the world can overcome poor service and poor attitudes."

This same principle applies to the church as well as the business world. People may initially be attracted to good and effective marketing. They may also be impressed by our products, our preaching, or our worship team. But all this will be undermined if we fail to maintain a positive attitude and a caring atmosphere, so that people sense that we're committed to serving them.

Inevitably, our attitudes create environments and then atmospheres. How many times have you gone to a store or other business—such as the supermarket, the DMV, or the post office—and someone's attitude was so bad that you never wanted to go back? Thankfully, we can do better than that in our churches or Christ-centered businesses. We can allow the peace of Christ to rule in our hearts (see Colossians 3:15), enabling us to keep a right attitude and right perspective. Instead of reflecting the negativity around us, we can manifest the presence of God and dispense the fragrance of heaven. (See 2 Corinthians 2:14–17.)

Thermometer or Thermostat?

I've found that many people—even Christian leaders—are content to simply reflect the atmosphere around them. If times are good, they have a good attitude. But if they're facing criticism or difficult circumstances, they allow their attitude to turn negative and toxic, mirroring the atmosphere around them.

This is much like how thermometers and thermostats work. Thermometers merely reflect the temperature around them. Instead of being change agents, they just tell you about the surrounding atmosphere. Thermostats, on the other hand, *change* the temperature in the room. When the atmosphere is cold, they trigger heaters to turn on. They create warmth.

PROVOKE-A-THOUGHT:

"DON'T LET THE NEGATIVE ATTITUDES OR SLANDER FROM OTHERS WASTE YOUR TIME AND DEPLETE YOUR ENERGY. IT WILL DISTRACT YOU FROM INVESTING YOUR TIME AND ENERGY ON WHAT IS MOST IMPORTANT IN YOUR LIFE, FAMILY, CALLING, AND VISION."

What about you, my friend? Are you like a thermometer, with attitudes that rise or fall according to the climate around you? Or are you a change agent, bringing constructive, healing attitudes to every situation you are in? When relationships, congregations, or businesses get too heated, do you have a gift for cooling them down? Or do you heat up with them?

No matter what you go through, your eyes should be on the Lord, and your perspective should be that He is bigger than your difficult circumstances. As you learn to abide in His peace and experience His presence amid adversity, you will find our lives bringing transformation to the people and the situations around you. Keeping your own attitudes in check, you'll be able to lead others into their own place of victory, vision, and hope.

Attitudes That Undermine Success

Pastor Wayne Cordeiro started a church in Honolulu that has had a huge influence not only in Hawaii but throughout Asia. In his book *Attitudes That Attract Success: You Are Only One Attitude Away from a Great Life*, he tells an insightful story of how success can be undercut by bad attitudes:

> The Los Angeles branch of the Bank of America is housed in a multilevel building with a parking structure on its lower floors. This large skyscraper housed many businesses. For many years, customers using the bank would not be charged for parking if they simply presented a ticket to the teller for validation with any transaction.
>
> Over the years, however, people began abusing this privilege by making small or insignificant transactions at the bank and then spending the rest of the day shopping at other businesses in the building. Due to the frequent infractions by shrewd customers, the bank reluctantly discontinued the privilege of validating tickets for free and unlimited parking. Validated tickets would henceforth be charged at a discounted hourly rate.
>
> One morning, an elderly man dressed in jeans and a flannel shirt waited his turn in a long line of customers. The line slowly inched its way forward, until he made his way to the next open teller's booth. The man made a small deposit and presented his parking ticket for validation. The teller stamped his ticket and informed him that he would have to pay a small amount for the parking.
>
> "Why? You've never required this before," the elderly customer replied.
>
> The teller, faced with a crowded bank full of impatient customers, snapped, "Well that's the new rule. I don't make 'em. I just dish 'em out."
>
> "But I've been a customer in this bank for many years," the man persisted. "The least you can do is validate it like you used to."

"You heard me, Mister. You got a problem with that, see the manager. I have a lot of people waiting behind you. If you could move along, that would make this morning go by a little easier."

The flannel-shirted gentleman made his way to the end of the long line of waiting customers, and once again he inched his way back toward the tellers' booths. When he finally arrived, he approached the first available teller, withdrew $4.2 million and went across the street and deposited it in another bank.[17]

The moral of the story? The teller's disparaging attitude cost the bank a $4.2 million withdrawal. Cordeiro warns us to never underestimate the destruction that can be wrought by a poor attitude. I bet that the elderly man wasn't as offended with the change in policy as he was with the disrespectful way he was treated.

How This Applies to Us

In the same way, a sign hanging on the wall of an old gas station holds a poignant truth.

Why Customers Quit

+ 1 percent die

+ 3 percent move

+ 5 percent leave because of location

+ 7 percent quit because of product dissatisfaction

+ 68 percent quit because of an attitude of indifference by one of the employees

Perhaps you're thinking, *But, Doug, what does any of this have to do with ministry and Christian leadership? The illustrations you've cited have to do with businesses, not churches or ministries.*

Yes, that is true. But if it's essential for businesses to display respectful, cordial attitudes toward their customers, how much *more* essential is it

---

17. Wayne Cordeiro, *Attitudes That Attract Success: You Are Only One Attitude Away from a Great Life* (Ventura, CA: Regal Books, 2001), 24–25.

for us Christian leaders to model warmth and respect toward those we're ministering to? Successful companies go out of their way for customers, even those who are angry and unreasonable. Shouldn't we as ambassadors of Christ outdo secular businessmen and employees? After all, God has filled us with His Holy Spirit and made us the recipients of His unmerited grace and favor!

You see, it's not enough to just treat people how they deserve to be treated. Thankfully, God didn't treat us that way, did He? No, the Bible declares that *"the goodness of God leads you to repentance"* (Romans 2:4). As we demonstrate that same kindness and grace, we will impact the world and lost people will be drawn to Jesus.

In a church setting, every person—not just the preacher—has a role to play in displaying the character of Christ. (See Philippians 2:5.) Even if the preaching and worship are good, people won't come back if they encounter church members with bad attitudes. Yes, customer service matters in businesses as well as churches.

Preparing for a Future Harvest

Wise businessmen and wise Christian leaders understand that sown seeds of respect and kindness do not always bring about an immediate return on investment. They recognize that they are sowing seeds for a future harvest. I've seen this principle demonstrated in some very surprising ways over the years.

From time to time, people will come up to me and ask, "Aren't you Doug Stringer?" When I ask how they know me, they say, "Oh, you shared the gospel with me one day when I was strung out on drugs, and Jesus changed my life."

My wife and I told our daughter, Ashley, that no matter where we go, we should always expect that someone will know us, and, therefore, to always be nice to people, even if they are being rude. Sometimes, people are just having a rough day and are in desperate need for someone to show them the love of Jesus.

In some of the strangest places, I've run into people who know me. Once it happened in a Chick-fil-A drive-through, and another time when I was sitting in a German airport. So no matter where you are, it's important to be Christlike, since you're His representative. You can't afford to display a bad attitude, especially if you're a leader. Every word, every action, and every attitude is a seed that will impact your future.

PROVOKE-A-THOUGHT:

"SOME POSITIONS CAN BE EARNED, BUT THE COMMISSIONING OF GOD IS CALLED FORTH BY APPOINTMENT. THERE ARE ELECTED OFFICIALS AND POSITIONS, THEN THERE ARE APPOINTED POSITIONS. WE CANNOT APPOINT OURSELVES, NO MATTER HOW MUCH WE WANT OR TRY. WE CAN ONLY ACCEPT OR REJECT THE APPOINTMENTS GOD GIVES US."

13

The Power of
Kingdom Vision

One of the indispensable requirements for successful leadership is vision. Jesus criticized the religious leaders of His day, saying, *"They are blind leaders of the blind. And if the blind leads the blind, both will fall into a ditch"* (Matthew 15:14).

Likewise, God instructed the Israelites to not allow anyone who was blind or had any other defect to be a priest. (See Leviticus 21:16–20.) This principle applies to us leaders today. It is impossible to lead others if we are blind or have blurry or distorted vision.

We also see a similar story in 1 Samuel 11. A general named Nahash the Ammonite came and encamped against the Israelites. The name Nahash literally means "serpent," a parallel with the tempter of Adam and Eve in Genesis 3. Nahash the Ammonite was a descendant of Lot, so you can imagine what a slimy, destructive person he was.

Not wanting to be annihilated by Nahash, the Israelites proposed that he make a covenant with them and that they would serve him. But Nahash was too wicked to offer any kind of reasonable terms to such an agreement. He replied, *"On this condition I will make a covenant with you, that I may put out all your right eyes, and bring reproach on all Israel"* (1 Samuel 11:2).

There were two important repercussions of Nahash's demand on the Israelite men.

1. Without a right eye, the men would be severely hampered in going to battle.[18] The loss of a right eye would make military service virtually impossible, since the soldier's right hand usually held the weapon and the sight of the left eye would be hindered by his shield. Unable to see the enemy, the soldier would be worthless.

2. As Nahash openly stated, this would *"bring reproach on all Israel."*

PROVOKE-A-THOUGHT:

"PERCEPTION IS NOT NECESSARILY THE TRUTH, BUT IT IS THE TRUTH TO THE ONE WHO PERCEIVES IT."

In the same way, great reproach comes upon the body of Christ when leaders lose their vision and don't finish the race well. What a stunning picture this story provides of leaders who've lost their vision and their sense of direction. No wonder Scripture tells us, *"Where there is no vision, the people perish"* (Proverbs 29:18 KJV). This is aptly paraphrased in *The Message*, *"If people can't see what God is doing, they stumble all over themselves."*

Seeing Jesus

Indeed, we need vision. Who sits at the right hand of the Father? Jesus! As we are told in Scripture, He *"sat down at the right hand of the Majesty on high"* (Hebrews 1:3). He is our right eye of righteousness, and if we build on anything other than Him, we'll never experience the fullness of His desires for us.

If we take Jesus out of the mix, attempting to battle on our own, we are bound to be defeated. The Bible gives us numerous promises of overwhelming victory over the enemy, but this victory is found only *"in Christ"* and *"through Him"*:

Thanks be to God who always leads us in triumph in Christ, and through us diffuses the fragrance of His knowledge in every place.

(2 Corinthians 2:14)

---

18. Flavius Josephus, *Antiquities of the Jews*, 6.5.1.

In all these things we are more than conquerors through Him who loved us.   (Romans 8:37)

He who is in you is greater than he who is in the world.   (1 John 4:4)

The book of Acts shows that there's no salvation, healing, liberation, freedom, or deliverance except in the name of Jesus. We desperately need His presence and power in our lives if we are to live in victory and finish the race well. The only way to withstand the storms, floods, and winds of life is to build on the foundation of Christ and His finished work on the Cross.

However, many people try to remove Christ from Christianity, leaving only a set of rules and moral precepts. Instead of genuine Christianity, we see something more akin to "X-ianity"—"*a form of godliness but denying its power*" (2 Timothy 3:5). And instead of keeping Jesus in the center of His church, we too often replace Him with rituals, potlucks, and spaghetti dinners.

Dr. Richard Halverson, former chaplain of the U.S. Senate, once made this sobering analysis of church history:

> In the beginning, the church was a fellowship of men and women centering on the living Christ. Then the church moved to Greece, where it became a philosophy. Then it moved to Rome, where it became an institution. Next, it moved to Europe, where it became a culture. And, finally, it moved to America, where it became an enterprise.

In order to fully impact the world, we need more than a nice philosophy or institution. Likewise, X-ianity, Christianity without Christ, will never turn the world upside down as the early apostles did. (See Acts 17:6–7.) And God forbid that the world would see us as merely a financial enterprise rather than a powerful movement of God's Spirit!

There's no substitute for an intimate, interactive relationship with the living God, our heavenly Father. Nothing else will release the authority, power, and favor of heaven upon a lost and needy world.

Kingdom Vision

Over the years, a statement I coined has been often quoted by others: "While men reach for thrones to build their own kingdoms, Jesus reached for a towel to wash men's feet." Every true leader has a vision of some kind or another, but not every leader has a vision to build the kingdom of God. Jesus showed how to build the kingdom of God when He reached for a towel to wash people's feet. Too many leaders throughout history have reached for thrones to build their *own* kingdoms instead of His.

If we truly have a kingdom vision, we will pay attention to the example of Jesus rather than the examples of ministry superstars. Success in ministry is defined as being like *Him*! Our Lord Jesus left His exalted place in heaven to seek the least and the lost (see Luke 19:10), while some leaders today seem intent on avoiding earthly discomfort and gaining bigger platforms to exalt themselves in the eyes of others.

Leaders with kingdom vision know that God's plans are bigger than themselves. Yes, God may call them to build great churches, tall buildings, and successful businesses, but at the end of the day, it's all about being God's ambassador and building His kingdom. They know they've been given a cause and mission infinitely bigger and more important than themselves.

When Peter and his friends were blessed with the miracle catch of fish, they had to work together to bring them in to shore. (See John 21:1–14.) That's a great picture of the harvest God wants to reap for His kingdom at the end of the age—a harvest so massive we'll need all hands on deck to bring it in.

Another intriguing detail in this account is the number of fish they caught—exactly 153. This is significant because, at the time, there were 153 known nations in the world. Three years earlier, Jesus had told Peter he would one day be a fisher of men. (See Mark 1:16–18.) Now, in this encounter with Jesus and the abundant catch of fish after the resurrection, Peter could see that the task before him was great. He and Jesus' other followers were called with a kingdom vision to go and "*make disciples of all the nations*" (Matthew 28:19).

I don't know anything about the vision you have for your life today, but I can tell you that it is too small! How could I possibly know that? Because a kingdom vision is bigger than you could ever dream or imagine. (See Ephesians 3:20.)

An Example of Kingdom Vision

Jon Brovold's business card describes his company, J.E.B. Enterprises, as a place "where sports and ministry meet." He travels throughout the year from city to city, for one to two weeks at a time, setting up temporary retail outlets at major sporting events, such as the Super Bowl, the College World Series, college football bowl games, the Final Four, and several NASCAR events.

In 1997, the Lord gave Jon a vision to use his business as a way to facilitate ministry. "It started when I began meeting people serving as missionaries with Youth With A Mission," he recalls. "That's when I saw people who were living lives of sacrifice, committed to serving God, and I realized I could be using my business to honor God as well."

Jon has a core team of individuals who travel with him as needed and available, but he also hires local missionaries as a way to provide them with financial support. He has donated facilities for outreach and coffeehouses in Houston, New Orleans, Phoenix, and other cities. He also contributes merchandise. In fact, when Somebody Cares contacted Jon for donations of sweatshirts for YWAM Houston's Christmas outreach to street kids, he cleaned out one of his warehouses and sent us nearly fifty thousand dollars' worth of t-shirts, sweatshirts, and fleece.

I met Jon just prior to the 2004 Super Bowl in Houston. I had been praying for large facility where Somebody Cares could hold an outreach event that would impact Houston and all those from around the country and the world who would descend on the city for the game. It just so happened that he had rented a facility in the heart of Houston to use as a retail store for the event. The venue had more space than he required and he was looking for a ministry that could use the available portion as a coffeehouse for outreach into the community. An employee of Jon's mentioned the opportunity during a meeting I attended, and soon Somebody Cares was introduced to J.E.B. Enterprises, and a beautiful relationship was born.

By the last week of January, a portion of Jon's store became our "outreach central" for the Super Bowl. Hundreds of visitors received coffee, snacks, and even meals at no charge. They listened to Christian musicians, received prayer along with free books and literature, and witnessed a tangible expression of Christ through our ministry's staff and volunteers. The location also served as a base for teams to disperse throughout the city for street evangelism. But it was all made possible through Jon's vision: Creating a partnership so that his marketplace ministry could become a part of sustained transformation in a community by working alongside local compassion and outreach ministries. But it hasn't all been a bed of roses.

In 2015, Jon's wife, Beth, had a vision to build on this foundation by creating an official ministry division of J.E.B. Enterprises that would develop and oversee intentional and strategic outreaches in conjunction with J.E.B.'s event operations. But around that same time, the Brovolds' business was battling serious financial challenges. "After some money-losing events and other circumstances beyond our control, we found ourselves in a very deep financial hole," Beth explains. "For several years I was not able to take a paycheck from J.E.B., and Jon only received eight or nine checks per year."

The Brovolds were forced to make some difficult financial adjustments, but God continued to see them through. That summer, they were faced with the possibility of losing their business, their house—everything. But God provided for them in miraculous ways and J.E.B. continued on. "At times," Beth says, "He provided for us in ways we can't even explain."

By keeping their eyes on a vision of hope, the Brovolds were able to persevere. "The fact that God made it clear that the ministry would be functioning as part of J.E.B. helped us to trust that He would somehow provide a way to keep the business going," Beth recalls. "That's not to say we weren't fearful at times, but we continued to remind ourselves that God never goes back on His Word. Never!" (See Hebrews 10:23; Psalm 33:11.)

Today, their new ministry is called Refreshed Tent Ministries, based on Proverbs 11:25: *"those who refresh others will themselves be refreshed."* J.E.B. introduced the inaugural outreach for Refresh Tent Ministries at the 2016 Final Four in Houston, using partners from Somebody Cares Houston and utilizing a booklet I wrote, *Who Was Jesus?*, along with other ministry resources.

"In looking back," Jon says, "we now recognize that God has been pre-paring us for something bigger than just J.E.B. He has been refining us and helping us to let go of what we viewed as 'needs' and turn our entire focus to needing only Him and trusting Him to provide for us. It has not been an easy journey—and it continues to be challenging at times—but we are bet-ter for it and honestly grateful for it. We rejoice in all that God has done in us these past few years (and what He continues to do), and we look forward to seeing what He is going to do through us in the future. God is *good!*"

He Bought the Whole Field

I find that many Christians have never given much thought to Jesus' story about the treasure hidden in the field.

Again, the kingdom of heaven is like treasure hidden in a field, which a man found and hid; and for joy over it he goes and sells all that he has and buys that field.   (Matthew 13:44)

Many people misread this passage, assuming that the man sold all he had in order to buy the treasure. But that's not exactly what it says. The man not only bought the treasure—he bought the entire field!

Do you see the distinction? Likewise, Jesus not only "sold all that He had" by laying down His life to purchase precious men and women—the treasure—for God's kingdom. In the process, He also bought the entire field! That means He is the rightful Owner of everything, including each of the seven mountains of society—business, government, media, arts and entertainment, education, family, and religion.

Scripture declares, "*The earth is the* LORD's, *and all its fullness, the world and those who dwell therein*" (Psalm 24:1). There are two reasons why the whole earth—including your city and neighborhood and every person in them—belongs to the Lord. First, He created the earth and each person on it, and for that reason He has a just claim to rule over them. Second, the Lord purchased the earth and all people who accept His salvation on the Cross.

This will change how you see the people you meet. God has a right to the allegiance of every man, woman, and child, because He created them, and He offers redemption to them through His Son. When you approach people with the gospel, you can boldly share that God is their Creator and that He offers them eternal salvation through Jesus' death and resurrection.

The story of the treasure hidden in the field reveals several important paradigms often missed by Christians today. Traditionally, Christians understand evangelism only in terms of reaching individuals. While this is an important aspect of the Great Commission, a kingdom vision goes even further, recognizing that God desires to reach entire nations and transform entire cultures.

So I pray you'll ask God to give you a bigger vision—a *kingdom* vision. Jesus died not only to save individuals and birth the church but to save the entire cultural "field" we find ourselves in. The ultimate purpose of God's kingdom is to fill the whole earth with God's glory. (See Habakkuk 2:14.) We can't allow ourselves to be boxed inside a stained-glass "ghetto," content with feeling holy goose bumps in our church services. We have a much bigger calling.

Those called to be lights on one or more of the seven mountains of society are often misunderstood and undervalued by those primarily called to minister in the church. But their ministry in these sectors of society is a crucial part of a kingdom vision. Scottish preacher George MacLeod put it this way:

> I simply argue that the Cross should be raised in the center of the marketplace as well as on the steeple of the church. I am recovering the claim that Jesus was not crucified between two candles, but on a Cross between two thieves; on the town's garbage heap; at a crossroads, so cosmopolitan they had to write his title in Hebrew, in Latin, and in Greek. At the kind of place where cynics talk smut, and thieves curse, and soldiers gamble. Because that is where He died. That is what He died for. And that is what He died about. And that is where church people ought to be, and what church people ought to be about.[19]

So let us continue to reclaim individuals and churches for the kingdom of God, but let's not stop there. We must also boldly take the kingdom into the marketplaces of our society, reaching our cities and penetrating every sphere of human endeavor.

19. George MacLeod, quoted in George Bloomer, *Elephants in the Church: Courageously Confronting Today's Tough and Controversial Issues* (New Kensington, PA: Banner Publishing, 2014).

14

Courage to Change the World

O ne of my favorite Leonard Ravenhill quotations deals with the challenge we face in living godly lives in an ungodly world:

The greatest miracle that God can do today is to take an unholy man out of an unholy world, and make him holy, then put him back into that unholy world and keep him holy in it.

Today, many Christians are quite confused about how they should live in the surrounding culture. The concept of being in the world but not of the world is frequently misunderstood. Look at how Jesus described this when praying to the Father shortly before His crucifixion:

I am no longer in the world, but these are in the world, and I come to You. Holy Father, keep through Your name those whom You have given Me, that they may be one as We are. While I was with them in the world, I kept them in Your name. Those whom You gave Me I have kept; and none of them is lost except the son of perdition, that the Scripture might be fulfilled. But now I come to You, and these things I speak in the world, that they may have My joy fulfilled in themselves. I have given them Your word; and the world has hated them because they are not of the world, just as I am not of the world. I do not pray that You should take them out of the world, but that You should keep them from the evil one. They are not of the world, just as I am not of the world. Sanctify them by Your truth. Your word is truth. As You

sent Me into the world, I also have sent them into the world.
(John 17:11–18)

Over the centuries, some Christian groups have erred on the side of totally withdrawing from the world. Jesus certainly didn't do this in His own life on earth, and He makes it clear in this prayer that He doesn't want His followers to withdraw themselves from culture, either.

Then there are Christians who embrace the opposite error, allowing the world to squeeze them into its mold. (See Romans 12:2.) Instead of being sanctified by the truth of God's Word, as Jesus prescribes here, these compromising Christians are blown around by the winds of political correctness. Sometimes, these fair-weather believers argue that lowering their standards makes them better positioned to reach lost people, so they can better relate to them.

However, the Bible is clear that we don't have to look like the world to win the world. In fact, the very opposite is true. Unbelievers are looking for authenticity, not compromise or hypocrisy. They are best won by Christians who display a sincere love and passion for the Lord, reflected in their godly lifestyles that stand out from others.

When I first got started in ministry, I didn't have to look like a street kid to reach street kids. I didn't have to become a drug addict to reach drug addicts. I didn't have to adopt a homosexual lifestyle to reach homosexuals, nor did I have to get AIDS to reach those with AIDS. Instead of trying to "fit in" with the group I was ministering to, I decided to be just who God called me to be; and I always found that Christlikeness has a bigger impact than compromise.

Loving the Sinner

Another area of confusion for Christians is how to hate the sin but love the sinner. Some Christians are so firm in their stance against gay marriage that they give the impression that they hate people who are trapped in the homosexual lifestyle. Though I hate sin and want to help people experience freedom, salvation, and deliverance, I never want anyone to get the mistaken impression that I hate him or her. We don't have to act like the world to win the world. Instead, we transform the world by modeling the characteristics of King Jesus.

Recently, Baltimore has been in the news for all the wrong reasons. It has become known for poverty, crime, and racial friction between community members and law enforcement officers. But our Somebody Cares affiliate in Baltimore has been hard at work in the community.

Several years ago, I was invited to speak there by the mayor and police commissioner. I shared some of the same principles I've described in this book, but I did so in such a way that I wasn't preaching at them. Instead, I was discussing time-tested values that could bring hope and transformation to both individuals and communities.

I also explained to the city leaders how the church and ministries like Somebody Cares can be their biggest assets instead of their biggest critics. I said that we're there to serve the community and show them practical solutions to difficult circumstances. You see, we can't just *preach* the answers to people; we must *demonstrate* the answers to people through our lives in tangible ways.

We started Somebody Cares Baltimore in one of its highest crime areas. At one time, it had been one of the country's highest murder and violent crime rate areas. It was a daunting situation, to say the least.

One of the first things we did was mobilize the local pastors to go out on prayer walks. This was a big step, but many of them pushed away their fears and started to "walk the beat" and intercede in this very dangerous part of the city. This sent a powerful message to the city that the church wasn't going to hide in a closet, so to speak. We were going to cross racial, ethnic, socioeconomic, and denominational lines in order to be the hands and feet of Jesus in the community.

Once the pastors began to get more involved as the salt and light in this troubled neighborhood, the business community began to take notice. "How can we help?" several business leaders asked. They ended up launching the Transformation Team, a group of law enforcement representatives, government officials, business leaders, and pastors who work to revitalize the community. It was stunning to see the secular community come together once the church leaders had taken steps toward positive change.

Note that secular community members did not ask the church leaders to compromise who they were. They respected and honored the Christian leaders for being themselves, authentically representing the kingdom of God. At the same time, the church leaders learned to drop some of their overly religious lingo, and became increasingly more Christlike in their actions.

The same basic scenario has played out in many other communities. In city after city, Somebody Cares and other ministries have demonstrated that Christians can make a significant difference through tangible acts of love and service outside of the four walls of the church. There's no need to compromise our convictions, but we must maintain the right attitude and reach out in sincere, unselfish love.

Isn't it good to know that we don't have to hide from the problems of the world? We can boldly take the presence of God with us, trusting in the same promise He gave to Joshua:

> *Every place that the sole of your foot will tread upon I have given you, as I said to Moses.... As I was with Moses, so I will be with you. I will not leave you nor forsake you. Be strong and of good courage.*
> (Joshua 1:3, 5–6)

In whatever sphere of society He sends you, you can take the sweet fragrance of Christ and live in victory. (See 2 Corinthians 2:14.)

Touching Your Enemies' Hearts

If I asked you what the best way to counteract evil in the world would be, what would you say? If you're like many people today, you may think of ordering drone missile strikes against terrorists or better surveillance to keep your countrymen safe.

Though our nation's leaders are sometimes called to use military force to bring peace and security, the Bible speaks of a much more fundamental approach: Changing the hearts of our enemies.

Here's how Paul described this revolutionary tactic:

Do not be overcome by evil, but overcome evil with good.
(Romans 12:21 NIV)

In the preceding verses, he had given some practical examples of ways to reach the hearts of your adversaries:

Do not repay anyone evil for evil. Be careful to do what is right in the eyes of everyone. If it is possible, as far as it depends on you, live at peace with everyone. Do not take revenge, my dear friends, but leave room for God's wrath, for it is written: "It is mine to avenge; I will repay," says the Lord. On the contrary: "If your enemy is hungry, feed him; if he is thirsty, give him something to drink. In doing this, you will heap burning coals on his head."   (Romans 12:17–20 NIV)

You might not think this idealistic principle could ever work in the real world, but I've seen its effectiveness countless times throughout my years of ministry.

In 1998, there was a major economic collapse throughout Asia. The collapse was particularly severe in Indonesia; over half the population lost everything. Suddenly, their money was virtually worthless. Can you imagine how devastating this would be? Families that had always had a roof over their heads found themselves living in garbage dumps and under bridges. Bad people became worse, and good people became bad. It was a very difficult and chaotic time.

In the midst of this craziness in Indonesia, some opportunistic people began to blame the Christians. Hundreds of churches were vandalized or burned down, and believers suffered many other atrocities. This was a lot like the days of the Roman emperor Nero, who stirred up trouble by blaming the Christians for burning Rome.

While all this was happening in Indonesia, a group of pastors invited me to come and speak to them. "Look," I said, "as hard as it is, we need to take the high road. That means reaching out even to those who misunderstand and abuse us."

In addition, I proposed setting up thirty-five feeding centers to hand out free lunches to the community. The pastors were skeptical, wondering if my recommendation would make the situation any better, and told me they had no resources for any kind of outreach. "Doug, you don't understand. We have no money!" they exclaimed. "The needs are enormous, and it's hard enough to provide help for our own people."

I didn't have a logical answer for them, but I told them there was one thing I knew for sure: God's Word is true, and He never asks us for what we don't have. All He asks is that we obey Him by giving of the time, talent, and resources we do have. "Look, I don't have an answer for how to do this," I said, "but I see the incredible impact it can have for God's kingdom."

As we discussed the options and tried to get God's perspective, I made my position clear: "I don't want to just come to your country, speak at a crusade, and then blow out of town. In order to do any good, we need to do more than just preach; we must give them something tangible." I went on to describe some times in my life when God had directed me to show kindness to enemies in order to reach their heart. I reminded them that preaching alone would not work. "You'll never be able to reach the heart of your adversaries by arguing with their minds," I told them.

Although they could see my point, they were still held back by their lack of resources. Any money they had saved in the past had become practically worthless—mere paper. It was the worst of all times for any kind of benevolent outreach.

"Okay, we don't have enough food or money to meet the needs we see," I admitted. "But remember the story of Jesus feeding the thousands of hungry people with a few loaves of bread and fish? He didn't ask for what His disciples didn't have; He asked them for what they did have. And, when offered in thanksgiving and prayer, their meager supply of loaves and fish became more than enough."

Well, God provided the resources for those thirty-five feeding centers in Indonesia, and the impact was so powerful that the president of the country invited me and one hundred Indonesian pastors to one of the presidential palaces. On national television, he made an astonishing statement, apologizing for how Christians had been mistreated: "To paraphrase your Jesus, 'Forgive us, for we know not what we do.'"

Let's be clear about this: On paper, you will never have enough resources to meet the needs God calls you to meet. However, when your heart is set on wholeheartedly serving the Lord and obeying His instructions, you will not just have enough—you'll have more than enough!

An Even Greater Impact

The free lunches had an impact beyond our wildest dreams. Even some of the people who had vandalized churches in the past had a change of heart. When they heard that someone was planning a new attack, they would rise up and say, "Don't touch that church. They care about us."

Little did we know that the free lunches would also position us for a far greater impact in December 2004, when Indonesia was struck by a devastating tsunami. By that time, we had credibility in the community, known for helping the poor and needy. When our team came to the aid of Indonesia after the tsunami, a number of the governmental leaders took notice. The governor of Aceh told our team that his mind and his heart were in conflict.

"Why is that?" our team asked him.

"When the U.S. was attacked on nine-eleven, we danced in the streets at your calamity," he explained. "But during our difficult calamity with the tsunami, you're not dancing in the streets. Quite the opposite, you're here to help us."

Do you see what an incredible impact we can have when we love and serve our enemies? And notice that transformation didn't come just through traditional evangelism and preaching. As St. Francis of Assisi beautifully said, "Preach the gospel at all times, and when necessary use words."

You see, there are times when people need to see Christ more than just hear about Him. They need to see the gospel lived out through us, as Jesus' hands and feet among the least and the lost.

This also applies to our sacrificial giving in the kingdom of God. I've met far too many Christians who begrudgingly give their 10 percent tithe, sometimes out of fear that they might be under a curse otherwise. But I'm convinced that the blessings of heaven aren't fully unleashed until we give more than just the minimum. Additional giving may include alms and sacrificial gifts to show the compassion of Jesus to the world.

A while after the tsunami, a former president of Indonesia visited the U.S. to attend a fundraiser for one of our ministry partners. Some leaders in her country had shared with her how Somebody Cares had been a huge blessing to Indonesia by sending resources in the wake of the tsunami. When she and I sat down in the lobby of her hotel, she began to pour out her heart about the ongoing needs in her country.

Finally, I stopped her and said, "Your Excellency, I don't know why you're telling me this. I'm small potatoes, just part of a tiny little organization that has a big heart and a lot of volunteers."

I was stunned by her reply: "You may be a small potato on paper, but you've helped our nation in very big ways through your relationship equities." What a great reminder that it's not about our size or our resources. It's about our obedience and God's blessing. As D. L. Moody once observed, "There are no limitations to what you can do if you've been in the presence of God and have gained His favor."

Days of Small Beginnings

The kingdom of God is meant to grow and to expand. (See Matthew 13:31–32.) For that reason, we're told not to despise our days of *"small beginnings"* (Zechariah 4:10 NLT), because they are just the beginning.

I have a friend named Suliasi Kurolo who is a pastor in Fiji. He started out in ministry with absolutely nothing. When I met him, he didn't even have a church. But God has used him in such a powerful way that now he has a church of several thousand people. He also started a Bible college and has hundreds of church plants around the world.

I marvel at how Suliasi never seems to have enough resources to do what he's doing. Yet he continuously applies the principles of God's Word by faithfully sowing into the lives of others, even when it seems he has practically nothing to give. He generously gives of his time, talent, and resources, choosing to trust in the Lord's economy rather than the world's economy.

What has been the result of his faithfulness to God and His kingdom? Suliasi always seems to end up with more than enough, and the Lord greatly multiplies his ministry.

Today, God is asking you and me the same question He asked Moses centuries ago: *"What is that in your hand?"* (Exodus 4:2). In all likelihood, it won't look nearly adequate to meet the needs we see around us. But in the Master's hands, it will be more than enough to reach a lost and needy world.

15

Becoming Faithful Stewards

When God looks for men and women to use in His service, He searches for people whose lives align with the gospel and His kingdom. He entrusts His resources to people who display the character of His Son, King Jesus. No matter whether a leader is called to pastor a church, manage a company, lead a nonprofit organization, or impact some other area of society, he or she is a sacred steward of God's resources and gifts.

If you're anything like me, you probably feel overwhelmed by God's calling at times. You're aware of your human frailty and limitations, and sometimes the challenges seem too great. Like the ten spies whose spines turned to jelly at the sight of giants in the Promised Land, you are tempted to cower in fear at the daunting mission set before you.

But there is good news. When God calls you, He also equips and empowers you to fulfill your mission. This beautiful Scripture puts this all in perspective: *"The eyes of the LORD move to and fro throughout the earth that He may strongly support those whose heart is completely His"* (2 Chronicles 16:9 NASB).

Notice that God doesn't support just anyone. He looks for a certain kind of person—someone *"whose heart is completely His."* Are you that kind of person? I surely hope so, because the Lord promises to *"strongly support"* the person who fully gives his heart to Him.

No matter what issues you face in life, remember this: The heart of the matter is always a matter of the heart. Why do traits like holiness, humility, honor, and honesty please the Lord and draw His favor? Because each of those characteristics is an indication that we've given our hearts to Him.

However, there's something I need to clarify before we move on. I'm not talking about perfection here. You may stumble and bumble along the way, but that doesn't mean you're hopeless! Biblical leaders from Noah to Peter failed terribly in their lives, but God still used them to fulfill His purposes. "*Though the righteous fall seven times, they rise again,*" Solomon wrote, "*but the wicked stumble when calamity strikes*" (Proverbs 24:16 NIV).

Think of King David. Despite his tragic fall into adultery and even murder, God said, "*I have found David the son of Jesse, a man after My own heart, who will do all My will*" (Acts 13:22). Once again, the Lord looked beyond David's outward appearance and saw his heart. (See 1 Samuel 16:7.)

If you've fallen and dismally failed the Lord in some way, it's time to "*rise again.*" There's still time to realign your heart and your life with His kingdom purposes. It's not too late to attract His presence and favor.

Faithful, Available, and Teachable

You've probably heard the old maxim "God isn't concerned about your *ability*, just your *availability*." There's a lot of truth in that statement. The Christian life is a supernatural life—God will gladly supply the *super* if we are willing to make available the *natural*.

Too often, ministry leaders are prone to select apprentices based on personality or giftedness. But look at Paul's instruction to his spiritual son Timothy on how to pick the next generation of leaders:

> *The things that you have heard from me among many witnesses, commit these to faithful men who will be able to teach others also.*
> (2 Timothy 2:2)

You see, one of the most important qualities of a leader is faithfulness. If you want to pour your life into the next generation, look not for those with spiritual gifts and charisma. Instead, be on the lookout for men or women who are FAT: faithful, available, and teachable. Faithfulness will trump flashiness every time.

And here's the good news about ability: When we are faithful in our walk with God, making ourselves fully available to Him, and are teachable, He will always give us the ability to fulfill our calling. Paul describes this beautifully:

> We are confident of all this because of our great trust in God through Christ. It is not that we think we are qualified to do anything on our own. Our qualification comes from God. He has enabled us to be ministers of his new covenant. (2 Corinthians 3:4–6 NLT)

So if you doubt your qualifications for some ministry or career God has called you to, spend some time meditating on this great passage. On your own, you may be totally unqualified; but you're not on your own! As Paul says here, your qualification comes from God. He has enabled you to be His ambassador, a minister of the new covenant.

When you have this perspective, God can use you to minister to anyone. You won't be intimidated if He sends you to a professional athlete, a billionaire, a famous entertainer, or a government leader. Neither will you be too proud to show the compassion of Jesus to those who are homeless, addicted, or oppressed by demons. You can reach people who are on top of the world and those scrounging for food at a third-world garbage dump. You're ready to be God's faithful ambassador to both the "up and outers" and the "down-and-outers," because He has faithfully equipped you.

Equipped and Adequate

Years ago, the Lord spoke to me through His words to Jeremiah:

> Before I formed you in the womb I knew you; before you were born I sanctified you; I ordained you a prophet to the nations. (Jeremiah 1:5)

Jeremiah was not impressed by the powerful commission he had been given from God; instead, he protested that he was inadequate for the task: "Ah, Lord GOD! Behold, I cannot speak, for I am a youth" (Jeremiah 1:6).

Perhaps you are feeling much like Jeremiah—unequipped and inadequate for the mission God has called you to. Maybe you are protesting just as he did, or perhaps you think that the Lord will be impressed by your humility. Look at how God responded to Jeremiah's protest:

> *Do not say, "I am a youth," for you shall go to all to whom I send you, and whatever I command you, you shall speak. Do not be afraid of their faces, for I am with you to deliver you," says the LORD. Then the LORD put forth His hand and touched my mouth, and the LORD said to me: "Behold, I have put My words in your mouth. See, I have this day set you over the nations and over the kingdoms, to root out and to pull down, to destroy and to throw down, to build and to plant."*
>
> (Jeremiah 1:7–10)

When I first read these words, I was just a youth myself, but I sensed the Lord challenging me to quit looking at my youthful inexperience or other inadequacies. Instead, I needed to look to Him as my Equipper, the One who enabled me to do *"all things"* (Philippians 4:13) through His strength.

As I prayed about this, I heard God tell me, "If you never forget where you came from, I will send you not only to down-and-outers but also to presidential palaces and to the heads of state." At that moment, I couldn't care less about reaching any heads of state, but I never forgot God's promise to empower me to reach people in any strata of society.

The foundational lesson for all of us is this: When God calls you, He will also equip you. Fear not! He is going with you. (See Joshua 1:3–9.) So be bold as you step into your destiny, reaching out to all those He puts in your path.

A Guy Named Hollywood

One day when we were doing an outreach for street kids and homeless people in Houston, I was talking with a guy named Hollywood. He was a pretty rough character at the time, but I felt strongly led by the Holy Spirit to tell him, "Hollywood, someday you're going to be to me like Nicky Cruz was to David Wilkerson."

He had no clue who David Wilkerson and Nicky Cruz were; perhaps you haven't heard of them either. Wilkerson reached out to gangs in New York City, and Nicky Cruz was converted to Christ during his ministry. Cruz eventually had a powerful ministry of his own. Their story was told in Wilkerson's book *The Cross and the Switchblade*.

Hollywood was intrigued by my statement and wanted to know more. "So, who's this David Wilkerson, and who's this Nicky Cruz?" he asked.

That day was the beginning of a very interesting relationship between Hollywood and me. He was in and out of jail, but he enjoyed reading the books I gave him about Wilkerson and Cruz. Whenever he got out of jail, he would take other kids off the street and drag them to my office to hear the gospel. "Listen to what this guy has to say," he'd command them.

Hollywood knew there was something powerful about the gospel message, and he wanted the other kids to hear it. However, despite his efforts to expose others to the gospel through my ministry, something always kept him from fully surrendering to Christ.

One day I was conducting a citywide Bible study in a hotel, and one of his girlfriends showed up. She was really getting into the message and was enthusiastically engaging with the people; but all of a sudden, Hollywood came up to her and told her sternly, "It's time to leave. Let's go." This woman had birthed a few babies to Hollywood, and he treated her with complete disrespect, as if she were his personal plaything.

The girlfriend did not want to leave that meeting, and she told him so. "But Hollywood, I really want to hear what they have to say."

"No, we're going," he said, with mounting anger. "You're my property."

This resulted in such an altercation that onlookers were ready to call 911. I told them not to. Hollywood was a massive guy, almost twice my size, and his girlfriend was quite petite, but I managed to get in between the two of them. She hid behind me and continued to tell Hollywood to leave her alone, insisting that she stay at the meeting.

Not wanting to lose face or back down, Hollywood told me firmly, "Doug, I respect you, but if you don't get out of my way, you're going down, man!"

I used to do some boxing and wrestling, so I was tempted to resort to fisticuffs instead of negotiation, but right when things seemed ready to explode between us, I told him calmly, "Okay, Hollywood, just back off," and nudged him a bit. Though I'd barely touched him, Hollywood suddenly started swinging. So I went ahead and defended myself. More agile than Hollywood, I flipped him over, held him to ground, and then yanked him out of the hotel.

"You're bad, man. You're bad," he wailed.

I sat him down and said, "Hollywood, you know that God loves you. It would break my heart if something were to happen to you after investing so much into your life. Why are you so angry? Why won't you let us in? You know what we're telling you is true, so why won't you receive it? It will not only break my heart but also God's heart if you end up in jail again or, even worse, dying."

At that moment, I saw more brokenness in Hollywood than I had ever seen before. "You just don't get it, man," he said. "I know what you're telling me is true. I know you guys care about me, and I've never felt so much love in my life. But in the Christian world, I'm *nobody*. On those streets, I'm *somebody*. I'm Hollywood, and I own those streets."

One morning at 6 A.M., I got a phone call from a taxi driver. He had my number from a business card we used to give out, saying, "Somebody Cares 24 Hours a Day."

"Doug," the taxi driver said, "I don't know how to tell you this, but Hollywood was shot and killed this morning, just after 3 A.M."

I just couldn't believe it. Deeply grieved, I kept asking the Lord why He would allow us to plant and water so many seeds in Hollywood's life and then allow this to happen. I thought He had told me that Hollywood would be to me like Nicky Cruz was to David Wilkerson. What was going on?

The memorial service for Hollywood was filled with street kids, and many of them turned from their life on the streets and surrendered their lives to Christ. Although my heart still grieved over the loss of Hollywood,

I could see that many lives were indeed touched as that one seed fell into the ground and died.

Faithfulness Rewarded

I'm often amazed at how God works behind the scenes in ways that aren't always apparent on the surface. I experienced this one day not long after Hollywood's death.

A young lady came to see me. She had a pretty incredible story, having been on and off the streets for several years, and our ministry had been reaching out to her since she was thirteen or fourteen years old. She was now living for the Lord, but it took some time before the gospel seeds bore real fruit in her life.

When she visited me that day, she told me a side of Hollywood's story that I knew nothing about. "Doug, did I ever tell you what happened the night Hollywood was killed?"

"No," I said.

"He was going up and down the streets, showing us some tickets he had to go home to Chicago. He was planning to get off the streets of Houston and go where he could start a new life serving the Lord!"

Wow. At that moment, I saw that God had been working in Hollywood's life in ways I knew nothing about. It was quite an illustration proving that it's not up to us to pick the fruit before it's ripe. We're called on to sow seeds and fertilize the ground.

The Bible promises that if we are faithful, God will bring an increase. Paul saw this in how the Lord worked through his ministry and Apollos' ministry.

Who then is Paul, and who is Apollos, but ministers through whom you believed, as the Lord gave to each one? I planted, Apollos watered, but God gave the increase. So then neither he who plants is anything, nor he who waters, but God who gives the increase.

(1 Corinthians 3:5–7)

What a great principle. If we do our part, God promises to do His part, as well. But I'll be honest. When you invest your life into people—especially needy and broken people—your heart will be broken. Sometimes you will conclude that your labor of love is in vain and that your seeds will never sprout. At times like that, you need to find encouragement in God's faithfulness, reminding yourself about promises like this:

> *Dear friends, stand your ground. And don't hold back. Throw yourselves into the work of the Master, confident that nothing you do for him is a waste of time or effort.* (1 Corinthians 15:58 MSG)

You may not see immediate returns on your investment, but you're not investing for short-term reward; you're investing for a future harvest. Everything you sow today is preparing a greater harvest to come. So, every day, set your heart on sowing and watering seeds of kindness, compassion, and truth.

16

Overcoming Feelings
of Inadequacy

I admit, I often feel totally unqualified to do the things God has called me to do. I don't feel I have all the needed education or training. Sometimes I even question my giftedness and intellect. It seems incomprehensible that God would give me a worldwide ministry, and some days I can't help but feel inadequate.

Perhaps some of my struggle is due to my Asian heritage. Asians believe that even if you get twenty different college degrees, they're still not enough. If you go to the best schools and get the highest grades, you still have fallen short and need more. So I've always had to deal with feelings of inadequacy, but that has given me an even greater motivation to lean on the Lord for my adequacy. (See 2 Corinthians 3:4–6.)

There's such freedom in knowing I don't need to compete with or impress anybody else. I need only to be who God wants me to be, making myself available to Him every day. Remember, the Lord is not concerned about our ability but our availability. From the moment I gave my life to the Lord over thirty years ago, I've said nearly every day, "Lord, if You can do anything with someone like me, then I'll make myself available to You."

Perhaps you're like me, scratching your head from time to time and wondering why God would choose to use you. I'm acutely aware of my human limitations. I'm just an ordinary guy who has made himself available to God.

That may sound rather simplistic, but that's my secret in a nutshell. I am available to the Lord, asking for His strength to help me fulfill His purposes for my life. And each day, I endeavor to walk in obedience to His voice.

A Lesson in Availability

Luke tells a fascinating story about being available to the Lord:

Now it happened that while the crowd was pressing around Him and listening to the word of God, He was standing by the lake of Gennesaret; and **He saw two boats** *lying at the edge of the lake; but the* **fishermen had gotten out of them** *and were washing their nets.*

(Luke 5:1–2 NASB)

As this story unfolds, we see a *need* (large crowds) and an *opportunity*. That pretty much summarizes the situations we all face as leaders, doesn't it? The needs around us are usually overwhelming, but they present us with wonderful opportunities to trust the Lord and His supernatural intervention.

I love that there were two boats, both of which were available to Jesus to use. Why? Because *"the fishermen had gotten out of them."* What a great reminder that Jesus wants us to empty our lives so He can fill them. As we get out of the way and decrease, He is free to increase. (See John 3:30.)

Jesus got into Simon Peter's boat *"and began teaching the people from the boat"* (Luke 5:3 NASB). If you truly grasp what is happening here, you will never have to feel inadequate again. You see, there was nothing special about Peter's boat. It was simply a wooden boat, not much different than any of the others. What made it special that day was that Jesus was in it!

In the same way, you may not feel as though you have any special abilities God can use. But if you make your "boat," or your life, available to Jesus, great things can happen! He can teach, preach, heal the sick, cast out demons, show compassion on the homeless, and do an unlimited array of other things from your little boat!

Although the story is already exciting at this point, it gets even better when Jesus says, *"Put out into the **deep water** and let down your nets for a catch"* (Luke 5:4 NASB). The lesson here is important for every Christian leader. God may have used you in the past, but in comparison to where He wants to take you in the future, you've only been in shallow water. He is speaking a powerful message to you and me today: "It's time to head into deeper water. Yes, I've used you in the past, but you haven't seen *anything* yet!"

When he heard these words, Simon Peter was skeptical at first. Perhaps you are, as well. *"Master, we worked hard all night and caught nothing,"* he told Jesus, *"but I will do as You say and let down the nets"* (Luke 5:5 NASB). This is such a great picture of simple obedience. Despite the failures and frustrations of the past, we need to take courage and let down our nets one more time.

You probably know how the story ends. *"When they had done this, they enclosed a great quantity of fish, and their nets began to break"* (Luke 5:6 NASB). Wow. They had worked hard the night before but caught nothing. However, everything changed when Jesus came on the scene and gave them instructions.

If you were paying attention at the beginning of this story, you may have noticed something intriguing. Two boats were empty and available to Jesus, but He chose the boat owned by Simon Peter. Does that mean that Jesus may disregard us and choose someone else instead?

Well, yes and no. Indeed there will be times when we aren't used by God like we think we should be. But look what happened later in the story: *"They signaled to their partners in the **other boat** for them to come and help them. And they came and **filled both of the boats**"* (Luke 5:7 NASB).

What a beautiful ending. Both boats were available, and both boats were a part of this massive catch of fish. If you feel underutilized at the moment, don't despair. Keep seeking the Lord, remain available to Him, and make sure you have a servant's heart. If you do these things, it's only a matter of time before you will participate in a supernatural harvest of blessings.

Preparation for Greater Things

If you or I were the fishermen who witnessed the miracle catch in Luke 5, we probably would have concluded, "It doesn't get any better than this!" Verse 9 (NASB) says, "*Amazement had seized* [Simon Peter] *and all his companions because of the catch of fish which they had taken.*" However, although the fishermen had experienced something quite astounding, they would have been mistaken to conclude that this was the ultimate miracle of their lifetimes. Jesus told Simon Peter, "*From now on you will be catching men*" (Luke 5:10 NASB).

You see, the miraculous catch of fish wasn't the pinnacle of the disciples' success. They weren't going to sit around in their old age and say, "Boy, that was the greatest day of our lives." No, not at all. This experience was meant only to whet their appetite for a far great mission—becoming fishers of men and women!

Take a moment to consider how this applies to your own life and ministry. Has God used you in the past? That's great. Every past experience is part of a training process to get you ready for even greater fruitfulness to come.

So how can we prepare ourselves for greater blessings? As already mentioned, our usefulness in God's kingdom begins with our availability and obedience. Maybe we've been available and obedient in the past; even so, we need to allow the Holy Spirit to search our hearts on an ongoing basis, ensuring that we're still "*a living sacrifice, holy, acceptable to God*" (Romans 12:1). The final verse in this passage shows that the disciples were still available—in fact, even more so—at the end of this episode: "*They left everything and followed Him*" (Luke 5:11 NASB).

The story of the miracle harvest of fish is filled with so much drama that it's easy to overlook the themes of holiness and preparation. Before any miracles occurred, we're told that the disciples "*were washing their nets*" (Luke 5:2 NASB). In the same way, we can't expect to win many people to the Lord until we've allowed Him to do a deep cleansing work in our lives. (See Psalm 51:10–13.)

It's also stunning that Peter repented *after* Jesus had blessed him with this abundant catch. *"Go away from me Lord, for I am a sinful man!"* (Luke 5:8 NASB), he said. This is an important point I don't want you to miss. We may have been used by God in the past, but that doesn't mean we should be arrogant and enthralled by our own press clippings; instead, we should give thanks to the Lord and humble ourselves before Him.

The Upside of Inadequacy

The fishermen were taken from inadequacy and unfruitfulness to a sudden harvest of supernatural blessings. As they made themselves available and simply obeyed Jesus' instructions, they stumbled upon the amazing reality that God is *"able to do immeasurably more than all we ask or imagine, according to his power that is at work within us"* (Ephesians 3:20 NIV).

Feelings of inadequacy can be crippling at times, but they can be used for our good. As King David sang in Psalm 61:2, when our heart is overwhelmed by the challenges of this life, we can say to the Lord, *"Lead me to the rock that is higher than I."* Awareness of our own inadequacy reminds us of our dependency on the Lord. We can pray to God, as the old hymn says so beautifully, "I need Thee every hour."[20]

The Bible presents us with such a wonderful truth on this subject. On the one hand, Jesus tells us, *"Without Me you can do nothing"* (John 15:5). Notice that He didn't say, "Without Me, you won't reach your full potential" or "Without Me, you won't accomplish much." No, unless we are intimately joined to Jesus, the Vine, we will accomplish *nothing* and bear no fruit at all.

We'll accomplish nothing apart from Christ, but Philippians 4:13 provides the other side of the coin: *"I can do **all** things through Christ who strengthens me."* So there's no need to hang our heads in defeat, frustration, and inadequacy. With the power of the resurrected Christ in us, we are able to live in victory and fulfill every assignment God gives us!

Like Jeremiah, Moses, David, Paul, and many other leaders in the Bible, we may have plenty of excuses why God should choose someone else.

---

20. Annie S. Hawks, "I Need Thee Every Hour," 1872.

Yet the Lord sees something amazing in us, something He can use for His glory, just as He did in these biblical leaders.

+ Moses wasn't a great communicator, organizer, or administrator, but God overlooked his flaws and called him to lead a nation.

+ David was the runt of his family, and no one saw him as a future leader. Yet God saw something great in the shepherd boy, and knew he would be a man after His own heart.

+ Tamar, Rahab, and Bathsheba all were included in the genealogy of Jesus, in spite of some very dark pages in their past.

+ Paul described himself as *"a blasphemer, a persecutor, and an insolent man"* (1 Timothy 1:13), as well as the chief of sinners (see verse 15). Despite all this, Paul said, "[the Lord] *counted me faithful, putting me into the ministry"* (verse 12) through His abundant grace.

So what are you waiting for? If God could use people like this in a powerful way, in spite of their shortcomings, surely He can use you as well. It's time to drop your excuses! Stop procrastinating and dive into the call of God on your life.

17

Attracting God's Presence and Favor

In order to have the maximum influence for God's kingdom and walk in the fullness of our leadership potential, we must ask a very important question: What attracts God's presence and favor?

I'm sure entire books have been written to answer this question, but I want to keep it simple. Four qualities, which I call the four Hs, play a vital role in attracting the Lord's presence to our lives and His favor in our endeavors: *holiness, humility, honor,* and *honesty*. None of these traits comes easily or by accident in our lives. We need intentionality and persistence to develop them.

PROVOKE-A-THOUGHT:

"THE LIVES WE LIVE BEFORE WE ENTER THE PORTALS OF ETERNITY DETERMINE THE INFLUENCE WE LEAVE TO FUTURE GENERATIONS."

This is seen in Revelation 19, where we're given a picture of *"the marriage of the Lamb"* (Revelation 19:7 NASB) at the end of the age. You and I are part of the bride of Christ, and we're told that *"His bride has made herself ready"* (verse 7 NASB). In a beautiful picture of holiness, this passage goes on to describe the bride's apparel at the wedding: *"It was given to her to clothe herself in fine linen, bright and clean; for the fine linen is the righteous acts of the saints"* (verse 8 NASB).

As His bride, Christ wants us to walk in His authority. However, we must first make ourselves ready. This happens when we clothe ourselves with His righteousness and commit ourselves to walking in His holiness. God has *"predestined* [us] *to be conformed to the image of His Son"* (Romans 8:29), which should be the foundation of our spiritual authority.

If you're married, you probably remember how you behaved when you were courting your spouse. You wanted to get yourself *ready* for the love of your life, and that meant some upgrades in your behavior. When I first courted my wife, Lisa, I put cologne on for the first time in months, and I brushed my teeth a lot more often. In short, I did everything I could to make myself attractive to her.

Ladies, I bet you made some similar changes to impress the man of your dreams. The fact is, we all do things to make ourselves more attractive to other people. We'll do whatever it takes to prepare ourselves for a special relationship.

In the same way, shouldn't we go out of our way to be attractive to the Lord? Shouldn't we study the qualities that please Him and attract His presence?

A Servant Bride

I didn't get married until I was fifty-two, so apparently the Lord had felt I needed a *lot* of preparation before I was ready to marry Lisa. In my many years of singlehood, I'd had plenty of opportunities to ponder the types of preparation the bride of Christ needs in order to "make herself ready." If we can answer this question, we will know quite a bit about the kind of person God can use for His kingdom purposes.

Genesis 24 tells a wonderful story about Abraham sending out a servant to look for a bride for his son Isaac. Abraham was a picture of the heavenly Father, who would later send out the Holy Spirit to look for a bride for His Son, Jesus.

Abraham's servant had a long way to travel to find a suitable bride, for he wasn't allowed to choose one from among the Canaanites. When he came to the Mesopotamian city of Nahor at evening time, he made his camels kneel down by a well of water. It was the time of day when the women went to the well to draw water, and the servant knew there was a good chance one of them would give him a drink.

Now, the servant wasn't looking for an *ordinary* bride for Isaac. He wanted to find an *extraordinary* woman with traits above the rest. So here's how the servant prayed:

> Now let it be that the young woman to whom I say, "Please let down your pitcher that I may drink," and she says, "Drink, and **I will also give your camels a drink**"—let her be the one You have appointed for Your servant Isaac. And by this I will know that You have shown kindness to my master." (Genesis 24:14)

You see, Abraham's servant was looking for someone who would go the second mile. (See Matthew 5:41.) Are you that kind of Christian—that kind of leader?

When the servant saw Rebekah, a beautiful young woman, he followed his plan and asked her for a drink. She quickly and happily complied, but that's not all. She added, *"I will draw water for your camels also, until they have finished drinking"* (Genesis 24:19).

Perhaps it's hard for you to imagine what an amazing offer Rebekah was making. Each camel, parched from the long journey, could drink up to forty gallons of water—that's potentially four hundred gallons of water Rebekah drew for all ten camels! And this huge task took place at the end of the work day, without the benefit of a water faucet or a hose. Rebekah had to dip the bucket into the well over and over again.

Even if someone would be willing to exhibit this "beyond the call of duty" type of servanthood to bless some dignitary like Billy Graham or the pope, consider this: Abraham's servant was a complete stranger to Rebekah, and she not only gave the man and his camels a drink but also offered to keep giving the animals water *"until they* [had] *finished drinking"* (Genesis 24:19).

What a powerful example for us as Christian leaders. Rebekah not only had a servant's heart, she had a persevering heart. God is looking for leaders who are willing to sacrifice for others, even when it seems there is nothing to gain. In addition, He desires leaders who don't quit until the job is done.

Rebekah was beautiful in outward appearance, but her extraordinary character, her inner beauty, displayed through her sacrificial service, was what set her apart.

Seeds of Future Blessings

Sometimes, we forget that Rebekah's act of kindness and generosity was done with absolutely no knowledge of the incredible blessings it would ultimately reap. If you've been walking with the Lord for a while, you probably have similar stories.

Over the years, I've received countless e-mails, letters, and calls from people all over the world who have thanked me for things I don't even remember doing! A woman once wrote to me on Facebook, "You may not remember me, but you took me off the streets when I was in my twenties. You set me up to stay with some of the girls in your ministry, and I probably broke your hearts when I left and lost touch with you. But I want you to know that today I work with AIDS babies and orphans in India. The seeds you sowed back then were not in vain. They really did stick!"

Another man e-mailed me and said, "Are you the Doug Stringer who walked up to me at a bar at the hotel I was staying at? You sat next to me, ordered a soft drink, and began to share about Jesus. I thought you were crazy, some kind of Jesus freak. But instead of being all religious, you just talked to me to see how you could minister to me."

The man went on to write that he had totally forgotten about the incident until a year later, when his wife told him, "There's a revival going on at a church in Houston, and I'd like you to go with me." When she spoke those words, something happened in his heart, so he went with her to the revival service. It just so happened that I was speaking at the service that night, and God's presence was there in a powerful way.

When he saw me at the podium, the man was dumbstruck. "That guy walked into a bar to talk to me over a year ago," he told his wife.

This is a great example of the power of the seeds we plant. The man told me he doesn't remember a single word I spoke to him that night in the bar. He just remembered my willingness to sit down and be real with him about the issues of life. I simply took time to talk with him, and he saw the tangible reality of Christ's compassion in me.

I could share story after story like that, when I was given opportunities to minister to people who had nothing to give in return. God is no respecter of persons—He loves us all the same. (See Acts 10:34; Romans 2:11.)

It's unlikely you'll have an opportunity to give water to ten thirsty camels. Yet the Lord wants you to be on alert for other divine appointments—chances to share His love with complete strangers who may have nothing to offer you in return.

The Camels Are Coming

One of my chapters in my book *In Search of a Father's Blessing* is entitled "Camels in the Wilderness." It's based on the story of Rebekah watering Abraham's ten camels, and I related the camels to the new generation arriving on the scene. Like the camels Rebekah so willingly and valiantly served, some of these new arrivals are coming out of a long journey through the desert of life. They may be penniless and homeless; and like a bunch of sweaty camels, they may not look like us or smell like us.

Yet, like Rebekah, we will have a choice to make when this radical new generation arrives on our doorstep. Will we gladly serve them, showing them the kindness of Jesus? Or will we selfishly and arrogantly turn away—and so miss out on the opportunity of a lifetime?

I'm convinced that in my lifetime I'll see a "John the Baptist generation," who will be a voice crying in the wilderness. They may not fit into our image of respectability, but their message will be powerful nevertheless: *"The voice of one crying in the wilderness: 'Prepare the way of the LORD; make His paths straight'"* (Mark 1:3).

This radical generation won't be politically or culturally correct, but they will be responding to a sound from heaven. They may not always get it right, but that's why we will be there, to take them under our wings and encourage them, empower them, and strengthen them. Though they will be strangers to us, we're called to give them the "water" they need to quench their weary souls. And as we help pave the way for them, they will pave the way for a new revival that will sweep the world. It will be a multigenerational revival, and we all can play a vital role!

A Transformed Life

At the start of this chapter, I pointed out that holiness is one of the four traits that attract God's presence and favor. So how does that stack up with my description of a radical "camel" generation, who will come out of the wilderness and spark a mighty, worldwide revival?

Part of our problem is that when we hear the word *holiness*, we automatically think of external piety and religiosity. We debate things like long hair and short hair, long dresses and short dresses, and different translations of the Holy Bible to decide which is *most* holy.

But through some difficult encounters with needy people over the years, I've come to see that holiness is a lot more than the external niceties of proper church folks. Here is a story that illustrates this well.

Several years ago, a man named John Hazzard came to our ministry. He was addicted to pharmaceutical drugs, cocaine, alcohol, cigarettes, and more; and he had worked as a drug mule for the Crips and Bloods gangs to support his habits. John had been diagnosed with HIV, and his doctors said he had only three to six months to live. By just about any standard, he was a mess.

Reaching a point of desperation, he had gone to a number of churches and ministries for help. But over and over, he'd received similar responses: "We're really sorry about your situation, but we don't really know what we can do to help you."

Eventually, John found his way to our ministry, and was probably shocked by our approach to helping him. Our first priority wasn't to get him off drugs or alcohol or any of his other addictions. We realized that all those external problems were just his way of compensating for his inner emptiness. And since he had only a few months to live, we set out to find ways to serve *him*.

It was beautiful to see God's love touch the heart of this person who had nothing to give in return. As people from our ministry showed him honor and respect, the Lord began to deal with his pain and his emptiness. But for us, this meant looking past all sorts of external issues to reach his heart with the kindness of Jesus.

John wanted to start reading the Bible, but his reading ability was extremely limited. So we got him a tutor, and she began by teaching him to read with an illustrated children's Bible.

When I was invited to Houston Baptist University to speak to their evangelism students, I decided to take John Hazzard with me. Before I spoke, I told them I wanted John to speak and share a little bit of his testimony.

John shared a passage of Scripture, telling the students how his tutor had taught him to read with a children's Bible. He described how the doctors gave him no more than six months to live, but by then it had already been a couple of years. Although his words came out slowly and haltingly, his story was powerful and he had a commanding presence. By the end of John's sincere, heartfelt testimony, there was not a dry eye in that class.

You see, it's not about our ability or our oratorical skills. Powerful things happen when we strip away our outward facades and simply share God's Word and the wonderful things He has done in our life.

Instead of living just three to six months, John lived nearly four more years. During that time, he went on sixteen or seventeen mission trips. On numerous occasions, he prayed for the sick and saw God bring healing and other miracles. He also became my top intercessor, especially when I was on a ministry trip out of the country.

My eyes still get misty when I think of the transformation God brought to John Hazzard's life. As we simply served him and showed him unconditional love, we saw the Lord perform miracles in his life. All the ugly external habits broke off as he was transformed by God's amazing grace.

True Holiness

If your focus is on external piety, you're going to miss out on the true nature of holiness. First, you'll miss it in your own life, because you'll end up settling for a religious facade instead of the character of Christ. Like the hypocritical scribes and Pharisees of Jesus' day, you'll become...

> ...*like whitewashed tombs which indeed appear beautiful outwardly, but inside are full of dead men's bones and all uncleanness. Even so you also outwardly appear righteous to men, but inside you are full of hypocrisy and lawlessness.* (Matthew 23:27–28)

There is another unfortunate consequence of focusing on outward rather than inward holiness: You will miss out on the beautiful transformations possible for people like John Hazzard who exhibit very *unholy* traits.

When people met John's external needs, God worked inside of him. You see, true holiness is a matter of personal consecration of our hearts to the Lord. It means saying to Him, "Whatever You want is Yours. I devote myself fully to You and to Your purposes." What counts is not what we look like on the outside but rather our hearts on the inside. We should have a heart like David's, of whom God Himself testified, "*I have found David the son of Jesse, a man after My own heart, who will do all My will*" (Acts 13:22).

Make no mistake about it: When you invite God into your life, He must be more than just a Guest; He must become the *Owner!* He must hold the title deed and the right to everything you have and everything you are. True holiness means you've offered yourself to God as "*a living sacrifice, holy, acceptable to God, which is your reasonable service*" (Romans 12:1).

You can attract more of God's presence by allowing Him to do the work of holiness in your life. With the power of His Spirit and His transforming grace, you can walk in the beauty of holiness as you worship and honor Him. He will change you through and through, from the inside out.

18

The Power of Humility and Honor

In addition to holiness, humility is key in attracting God's presence and blessings. One of the reasons so many leaders insist on going it alone is because they have an overinflated view of their own abilities. This is an extremely dangerous condition, as pointed out by Robert Murray M'Cheyne, a minister in the Church of Scotland from 1835 to 1843: "There's nothing more deceitful than your estimate of your own strength." M'Cheyne was also quoted as saying, "Remember, you are not a tree, that can live or stand alone. You are only a branch. And it is only while you abide in Christ, as the branch in the vine, that you will flourish or even live."

That is true of each and every one of us. As Jesus warned in the gospel of John, you're only a branch, and you'll flourish and bear fruit only when you abide in Him. (See John 15:1–5.) This is true of each and every one of us. There are no exceptions. Only a delusional person would claim to be a "super-Christian," never needing anyone else.

Many Scripture passages point out the blessings of humility and the dangers of pride, and here is one of my favorites:

All of you be submissive to one another, and be clothed with humility, for "God resists the proud, but gives grace to the humble." Therefore humble yourselves under the mighty hand of God, that He may exalt you in due time. (1 Peter 5:5–6)

Peter was making three distinct points here:

1. God actively resists the proud.

2. God actively gives grace and favor to the humble.

3. When we humble ourselves, God promises to exalt us "*in due time*," which is not always immediately.

What a clear picture this paints of the pathway to God's favor. We're told what kind of attitude He resists, and what kind of attitude He blesses. Furthermore, we're reminded that even if we don't yet see God's fullest blessings, they will come in due time if we humble ourselves and patiently wait.

Before we go any further, I encourage you to pause for a moment and invite the Holy Spirit to search your heart on this issue. Have you humbled yourself "*under the mighty hand of God*"? If so, are you waiting patiently and expectantly for a new level of His favor in your life?

Humility Rewarded

David Robinson was one of the most successful NBA basketball players of all time. As the star center of the San Antonio Spurs, he was the league MVP in 1995, a two-time NBA champion, and a ten-time NBA All-Star. He also won two Olympic gold medals and received a wide array of personal accolades. Because of his prior service as an officer in the U.S. Navy, Robinson was fondly referred to as "the Admiral." After retiring from basketball, he has continued to impact society through his businesses, philanthropy, and ministry.

No doubt, David Robinson had a lot of God-given talent, but his success was based on more than talent alone. He was widely known for his humility and gracious demeanor off the court. Yes, he was good at what he did, and he trained hard to be the best he could be; but he didn't have a chip on his shoulder or have anything to prove. Other star players were known for their braggadocio, but not Robinson. Instead of trying to exalt himself or prove a point, he just operated within his skillset.

Along with countless other fans, I was drawn to David Robinson's humility and strength of character. He was Christlike both on and off the court, never tinged by the kinds of scandals many professional athletes have gotten themselves into.

In contrast, an NBA All-Star during the same era as Robinson openly boasted that he was no role model for America's young people. He was known for his partying lifestyle and for hanging out at Houston's topless bars. Although this man had an engaging personality, his character was marked by arrogance rather than humility.

So what does the Bible say about all of this?

By humility and the fear of the LORD are riches and honor and life. Thorns and snares are in the way of the perverse; he who guards his soul will be far from them. (Proverbs 22:4–5)

Again, we see a vivid contrast. If we want God's blessings—*"riches and honor and life"*—we will need *"humility and the fear of the LORD."* But if we reject these essential character traits, we are likely to reap *"thorns and snares."*

You see, each of us is a magnet either of God's blessings or His judgment. If we are fully aligned with the Lord and His kingdom, we will attract His favor; but if we reject godly qualities like holiness and humility, we will repel the blessings He wants to give us.

You have an important choice to make, as Scripture describes: *"If you are willing and obedient, you shall eat the good of the land; but if you refuse and rebel, you shall be devoured by the sword"* (Isaiah 1:19–20). So I encourage you to humble yourself before the Lord today. Choose to obey Him, and let Him give you His best.

A Heart of Honor

After holiness and humility, honor is the third ingredient necessary to attract God's presence and favor. Growing up in an Asian home, I had this drilled into me at an early age.

"Dougie, take your shoes off!" I can still hear my mother command, as if it was yesterday.

"Okay, Mom," I would reluctantly reply. "But we live in America now, and not everyone does it that way here."

There was nothing I could do to change my mother's mind on this. To her, it was a sign of honor and respect. One day, I tried to gently point out that she was living in *my* house and maybe I should set the rules.

"I don't care if it's your house," Mother said forcefully. "I raised you. I changed your diapers. So you need to do what I say and take off your shoes when you enter the house."

My mom was a short little lady, not even five feet tall. But she was incredibly tough, impossible to disrespect.

However, we still had run-ins on a number of other issues. Toward the end of my mother's life, she had a small Pomeranian dog with a bunch of fluffy fur. I didn't like having all the dog fur throughout my house, so I took the dog to get groomed.

"Dougie, that's not good," my mother told me, quite upset. "Pomeranians will die if their fur is cut."

"Mother, that's not true," I insisted. However, she was not persuaded. Finally, I got her to agree to go with me to the pet store to settle the issue. I asked the dog groomer, "If you trim this dog's fur down to almost nothing, will it die?"

"Oh, no!" the groomer assured us. But I'm still not sure my mother was fully convinced. She started getting a special haircut for the dog, leaving hair on its tail and a little mane on its head. As a result, it looked like a character out of *The Lion King*. Oh, well...

Mother and I also disagreed on whether Kleenex tissue would clog a toilet. "Kleenex and toilet paper are the same," I told her.

"No Dougie, they're different," she said confidently.

To my amazement, mom turned out to be correct. I saw a TV special that explained the differences between the two tissues, and warned against putting Kleenex in toilets.

There's a point to these humorous encounters with my mother: When we had a dispute, I could choose either to honor her or dishonor her. When we honor the people God has put in our lives—even when we disagree with them—a blessing is released.

I found that God released more of His favor in my life when I learned to honor my mom. Even when we disagreed, her words had an influence on me. I'll never forget the day some of my friends came over to the house after my mother had gone to be with the Lord. "Take your shoes off!" I told them as they came through the door.

Knowing that this had been a contentious issue between me and my mother, my friends replied with surprise, "But your mom's not around anymore."

"I don't care. Take your shoes off," I persisted.

You see, I could hear my mother's voice in my head. Even though she was now in heaven, I could hear the familiar words "Dougie, take your shoes off."

Someday, when I join her in heaven, I envision her meeting me at the pearly gates. "Dougie, take your shoes off," she will insist once again. "This is holy ground." I guess Mom was right all along.

So if you are from the emerging generation, I challenge you to honor and respect those who have gone before you. There's no better way to release God's blessings in your life, catapulting you into an awesome future. We are all the beneficiaries of the foundation that has been laid, the sacrifice that has been made, and the price that has been paid on our behalf.

Abusive Leaders

Whenever I teach on the importance of honor, someone always raises an excellent question: How are you supposed to honor abusive parents, bosses, or leaders in the church or civil government? I'll admit, this can be extremely difficult. Of course, I'm *not* advocating that anyone unconditionally or blindly follows an authority figure whose behavior is illegal, immoral, or unscriptural. (See Acts 5:29.) Nevertheless, we should strive to honor them, even when we disagree with them and how they exercise their authority.

This was a lesson I had to learn in dealing with both my stepdad and biological father. At times, their actions weren't deserving of my honor and respect, but I chose to honor them anyway. And the result? Both my stepdad and my biological father were saved and are in heaven today, partly because I honored God by respecting them.

I'm convinced that honor plays a huge role in intergenerational blessings, as well. If we honor the legacy of the generation before us, it's much more likely that the generation to come will honor our own legacy. However, if we dishonor the leaders who have gone before us, we are in danger of reaping disrespect from those who follow us.

This certainly isn't easy when leaders aren't very respectable; yet the Bible commands us to look for the positive rather than the negative. (See Philippians 4:8.) And we're told to demonstrate love so powerfully that it actually covers the sins of the people around us:

Hatred stirs up strife, but love covers all sins. (Proverbs 10:12)

Above all things have fervent love for one another, for "love will cover a multitude of sins." (1 Peter 4:8)

This principle is demonstrated quite graphically in Genesis 9, when Noah got drunk and lay naked in his tent. His son Ham saw his nakedness and immediately told his brothers, Shem and Japheth. These two brothers took a garment and covered their father's nakedness, and they made sure to turn their faces away, so that they would not witness their father's nakedness.

This story has a stunning and sobering conclusion. When Noah woke up, he cursed Ham's son Canaan, saying he would be *"a servant of servants"* (Genesis 9:25). In contrast, Noah spoke great blessings over his sons Japheth and Shem. The powerful lesson here is all about honor and dishonor. By dishonoring his father and revealing his nakedness, Ham reaped curses on himself and his descendants. On the other hand, Japheth and Shem received favor because they'd exhibited love and respect, covering Noah's sinful condition.

Which of these examples do you follow when you become aware of a leader's "nakedness"? Are you like Ham, eager to tell the world about your leader's sins? Or do you follow the example of Japheth and Shem, providing a covering of love, intercession, and restoration to those who have fallen?

Honoring the Lord

The same principles of respect hold true in our relationship with the Lord. We see this when God rebukes His people for dishonoring Him with second-rate, blemished sacrifices:

> "A son honors his father, and a servant his master. If then I am the Father, where is My honor? And if I am a Master, where is My reverence?" says the LORD of hosts to you priests who despise My name. Yet you say, "In what way have we despised Your name?" "You offer defiled food on My altar, but say, 'In what way have we defiled You?' By saying, 'The table of the LORD is contemptible.' And when you offer the blind as a sacrifice, is it not evil? And when you offer the lame and sick, is it not evil? Offer it then to your governor! Would he be pleased with you? Would he accept you favorably?" says the LORD of hosts. "But now entreat God's favor, that He may be gracious to us. While this is being done by your hands, will He accept you favorably?" says the LORD of hosts. "Who is there even among you who would shut the doors, so that you would not kindle fire on My altar in vain?...But you profane it, in that you say, 'The table of the LORD is defiled; and its fruit, its food, is contemptible.' You also say, 'Oh, what a weariness!' And you sneer at it," says the LORD of hosts. "And you bring the stolen, the lame, and the sick; thus you bring an offering! Should I accept this from your hand?" says the LORD. "But cursed be the deceiver who has in his flock a male, and takes a vow, but sacrifices to the LORD what is blemished—for I am a great King," says the LORD of hosts, "and My name is to be feared among the nations."   (Malachi 1:6–14)

Instead of honoring God as the "great King," bringing Him their best, the Israelites brought Him their leftovers: "the stolen, the lame, and the sick."

Although they claimed to seek God's grace and favor, their tawdry sacrifices dishonored Him.

Before we're too hard on the Israelites, we must examine our own life. Are we truly giving the Lord our best, or are we content in offering Him our spare money, time, and talents?

19

A Life of Honesty and Authenticity

The final quality that will attract God's presence and favor in your life is honesty, which is increasingly rare in our world today. The Bible is full of references to this important trait. Solomon says, *"Whoever walks in integrity walks securely, but whoever takes crooked paths will be found out"* (Proverbs 10:9 NIV). In a parallel passage, he adds, *"He who is crooked in his ways will suddenly fall"* (Proverbs 28:18 ESV).

These verses provide an incredible contrast between people who walk in honesty and integrity and people who walk in crookedness and deceitfulness. We're promised security and safety when we're honest; but if we take *"crooked paths,"* our sins will eventually be exposed and we're likely to *"suddenly fall."*

No wonder so many leaders fail to finish well. They may look successful on the outside, but lack of integrity eventually leads to their demise. Dishonesty undermines the very foundation of our lives, leaving us vulnerable to every passing storm.

Prison Fellowship founder Charles "Chuck" Colson once observed, "We must be the same person in private and in public. Only the Christian worldview gives us the basis for this kind of integrity." Take a moment to let these words sink in. Are you the same person in private and in public? Or are you two-faced—engaging in dishonesty, flattery, and misrepresentations of who you really are?

I've been a part of many large gatherings of Christians throughout the years, and often they have been a huge personal blessing. God's presence comes when His people join together in united worship and prayer. But at times, I've seen a big gap between the public and private lives of the leaders who take the stage at such events. Some have great oratorical skills and can utter impressive prayers in public. Yet God isn't primarily looking for leaders who can inspire a crowd, but rather people whose prayers can shake the gates of heaven.

Let's be honest: We all can come up with good prayers every once in a while in a large gathering. But Christian leaders need to know how to pray in private, because prayerlessness in private will always result in powerlessness in public.

When a man or woman of God prays earnestly in private, he or she will have a great impact when praying, preaching, or teaching in public. People will sense the presence of the Lord and the conviction of the Holy Spirit. However, if a person does not have an authentic prayer life, he or she can speak the same message as a David Wilkerson or Leonard Ravenhill, but people will be unaffected or may even feel beaten down. Transformative public ministry must be preceded by powerful, anointed private prayers.

When God Rejects Our Sacrifices

Scripture vividly shows God's disdain for empty religious exercises—even worship and prayer—when our private lives are not properly aligned with Him.

Quit your worship charades. I can't stand your trivial religious games: Monthly conferences, weekly Sabbaths, special meetings—meetings, meetings, meetings—I can't stand one more! Meetings for this, meetings for that. I hate them! You've worn me out! I'm sick of your religion, religion, religion, while you go right on sinning. When you put on your next prayer-performance, I'll be looking the other way. No matter how long or loud or often you pray, I'll not be listening. And do you know why? Because you've been tearing people to pieces, and your hands are bloody. Go home and wash up. Clean up your act. Sweep your lives

clean of your evildoings so I don't have to look at them any longer. Say
no to wrong. Learn to do good. Work for justice. Help the down-and-
out. Stand up for the homeless. Go to bat for the defenseless.
(Isaiah 1:13–17 MSG)

Strong language, wouldn't you say? The Lord says He doesn't see genuine spirituality but worship charades, trivial religious games, and special
meetings and conferences. His people were pious in public but were sinning behind the scenes. No wonder God wasn't impressed by their "prayer
performances."

God's advice in Isaiah, hundreds of years before Christ, is fitting for
us today: "*Go home and wash up. Clean up your act. Sweep your lives clean*
of your evildoings" (Isaiah 1:16 MSG). And the Lord adds that if our faith is
sincere, we'll "*work for justice. Help the down-and-out. Stand up for the home-*
less. Go to bat for the defenseless" (Isaiah 1:17 MSG).

I get chills when I read these words. What would happen if we all took
this message to heart?

Lives of Integrity

Having integrity means that your public life and private life are consistent with each other. This doesn't come easily or automatically; you will
have to regularly spend time in the presence of God, allowing His searchlight to reveal any areas of hypocrisy, compromise, or inconsistency.

In order to consistently walk in integrity, you will also have to make
some important choices, as pastor and author Rick Warren reminds us:

Integrity is built by defeating the temptation to be dishonest; humility grows when we refuse to be prideful; and endurance develops every time you reject the temptation to give up.

The Bible says that the battle for honesty and integrity will intensify
in the last days:

The coming of the lawless one will be in accordance with how Satan works.
He will use all sorts of displays of power through signs and wonders that

serve the lie, and all the ways that wickedness deceives those who are per-
ishing. They perish because **they refused to love the truth** *and so be saved.*
For this reason God sends them a **powerful delusion** *so that they will*
believe the lie *and so that all will be condemned who* **have not believed**
the truth *but have delighted in wickedness.*

(2 Thessalonians 2:9–12 NIV)

According to this passage, the first step in people's downward spiral comes when *"they [refuse] to love the truth."* Notice that it doesn't say they were never exposed to the truth or never received the truth. Instead, it focuses on an issue of the heart: They failed to *love* the truth. Many people today love the truth only when it suits their purposes. They treat God's truth as if it's elastic, as if it can be shaped and molded to fit into their own plans and pursuits.

But look at the outcome of this relativistic manipulation of truth. Those who don't love the truth will ultimately embrace *"a powerful delusion"* and *"believe the lie."* Instead of building their lives upon the firm foundation of God's Word, they build their lives on the sands of personal preference and political correctness. Without a controlled rudder, they will be blown about by every cultural wind; and without truth, their minds will increasingly be filled with satan's lies.

How's Your Discernment?

In today's crazy world, Christian leaders need discernment more than ever before. And I'm convinced that discernment comes when we love the truth and are committed to speaking it.

The apostle Paul repeatedly spoke of his commitment to honesty and integrity in his life and his message.

The appeal we make does not spring from error or impure motives, nor are we trying to trick you. On the contrary, we speak as those approved by God to be entrusted with the gospel. We are not trying to please people but God, who tests our hearts. You know we never used flattery, nor did we put on a mask to cover up greed—God is our witness. We

were not looking for praise from people, not from you or anyone else.
(1 Thessalonians 2:3–6 NIV)

Unlike so many, we do not peddle the word of God for profit. On the contrary, in Christ we speak before God with sincerity, as those sent from God. (2 Corinthians 2:17 NIV)

Paul knew that those who deceive others will eventually fall prey to deception themselves. *"Evil men and impostors will grow worse and worse, deceiving and being deceived"* (2 Timothy 3:13). Dishonesty and deception always follow a predictable trajectory—growing *"worse and worse"*—unless they are ruthlessly eliminated from our lives.

The story of Jacob illustrates how those who sow deception will inevitably reap deception in their lives. Remember how Jacob deceived his brother, Esau, and later his father, Isaac? He was a con artist, plain and simple. So it was no coincidence that Laban tricked Jacob on several occasions. Jacob, the deceiver, ended up *"being deceived."*

So if you want to be a person of discernment, free from deception, there are two things you need to do: Love the truth, and commit to speaking truthfully to others.

The Power of Authenticity

I've been around some churches and ministries where there is a lot of hype but very little evidence of God's presence. Some pastors and musicians are virtual rock stars these days, and modern technology makes it possible to put on dazzling shows with sights, sounds, smoke, lights, and other special effects. I'm certainly not against excellence, but we need to value the presence and power of the Lord above all else.

On the other end of the spectrum, I've sometimes felt God's presence in awesome ways while listening to stuttering preachers and mediocre music. Perhaps you've had similar experiences.

Before A. R. Bernard was saved, an elderly lady where he worked invited him to hear Nicky Cruz, a former gang member, speak. Bernard didn't know anything about Nicky but he agreed to attend because the woman had been annoyingly persistent in inviting him.

When Nicky first started speaking, Bernard regretted being there. Nicky's accent was so thick that Bernard could hardly understand a word he said! However, that man was anointed by the Holy Spirit, and Bernard found himself desperately wanting the Jesus Nicky was talking about. He got saved that day! And it certainly wasn't because of Nicky's showmanship or human eloquence—it was *God's presence* that transformed his life that day.

Today Dr. A. R. Bernard pastors a church of more than twenty thousand people in Brooklyn, New York, and he impacts people all over the world. As he describes that pivotal moment in his life, he says he responded because Nicky Cruz was a lover of God, a lover of the truth, and a lover of people. Those were the qualities Dr. Bernard wanted in his own life, as well.

Whatever the cost, I want to attract and radiate the presence of the Lord wherever I go and in every word I say. I know that it requires brutal honesty with myself and with God—but it is worth the price.

Uncovering Hidden Sins

Hiding our sins never works. The Bible declares, *"Whoever conceals his transgressions will not prosper, but he who confesses and forsakes them will obtain mercy"* (Proverbs 28:13 ESV). In order to walk in honesty and integrity, we must confess our transgressions to the Lord and forsake them in the future.

But too often, we see our ministry peers publicly humiliated because they won't deal with their secret sins. Instead of privately confessing and forsaking their sins, they wait until the Lord publicly exposes them. This is not something God delights in doing; but sometimes it's the only way He can bring us to repentance and restoration.

Then there are times when we aren't even in touch with the sins that are lurking in our heart. That is a very common occurrence, and the only real solution is to cry out to the Lord to search our heart, as King David did:

Who can discern his errors? Acquit me of hidden faults. Also keep back Your servant from presumptuous sins; let them not rule over me; then I will be blameless, and I shall be acquitted of great transgression.
(Psalm 19:12–13 NASB)

This process is not just human introspection or spiritual navel-gazing. It's a matter of opening our heart to the searchlight of God's Spirit, enabling Him to reveal any wicked way or *"hidden faults"* we're unaware of.

Although God's dealings can be quite painful, I want Him to deal with any sin in my life. Don't you want the same? I want to be stretched. I want to walk in character. Although I often fall short, I want to be the man He has called me to be. I know I need His help do this, which is readily available when I honestly and humbly request it.

God is calling us to a deeper level of availability and obedience, and one of the first steps is to commit ourselves to complete honesty before Him!

20

Your Personal Consecration

Every Christian leader must determine his or her own level of consecration on the debatable issues of Christian life. But one thing is beyond debate: Your example matters. Regardless of the sphere of leadership you're in, people are watching, and they will inevitably be influenced by how you live your life.

Even Jesus had to purposefully consecrate Himself to set the proper standard for His followers: *"For their sake I consecrate myself, that they also may be sanctified in truth"* (John 17:19 ESV). Jesus consecrated Himself for two basic reasons: Because He loved His Father and wanted to please Him, and because He loved His followers, including you and me. These same motivations should still shape the decisions of every Christian leader today.

We see this same principle in the life of the apostle Paul. *"Follow my example, as I follow the example of Christ"* (1 Corinthians 11:1 NIV), he told the believers in Corinth. And he commended his spiritual son Timothy for following not only his teachings but his *"manner of life,"* as well: *"You have carefully followed my doctrine, manner of life, purpose, faith, longsuffering, love, perseverance, persecutions, [and] afflictions"* (2 Timothy 3:10–11).

I hope you are able to boldly tell people to follow your example, because you are confidently following the example of Christ. I hope your *"manner of life"* is consistent with the standards you profess and the teachings of the Scriptures.

Developing Personal Convictions

I desire to take personal responsibility to live according to the calling God has put on my life. Accordingly, I've set high standards for my conduct and lifestyle. I do not judge others by these standards—I've determined to never force my level of consecration to God on others—they are simply a matter of my own accountability before the Lord.

For example, I made a personal decision not to drink alcohol. I have many friends and Christian leaders who don't share this conviction, and I don't have a problem with their personal positions. I don't judge them; I just have a different conviction.

There are several reasons I've come to this personal conviction. First of all, I believe God has called me to be a forerunner. I want to always be clear-minded, exercising self-control. I don't want to open myself up to temptation, or allow anything or anyone but the Lord to control my life.

But there's also another reason for my choice not to drink alcohol—one that is highly personal. My father and my stepdad both were alcoholics, and I witnessed the devastating consequences that abusing alcohol or other substances can have on a person. While some people are able to drink in moderation, others can't, making alcohol abuse the biggest drug problem in America. Over the decades, I have had a ministry to young people who have looked to me as an example. For many, my liberties could become an excuse for their license, thus causing them to stumble.

PROVOKE-A-THOUGHT:

"WE NEED PRINCES, POLITICIANS, PRIESTS (PASTORS), PROPHETS, AND PEOPLE WHO LOVE GOD AND OTHERS MORE THAN THEY LOVE THEMSELVES. FROM PREACHERS TO POLITICIANS, FROM PULPITS TO POLITICAL OFFICES, AND IN BETWEEN, WE NEED *A REVIVAL OF CHARACTER!*"

Of course, I hear people say all the time, "Doug, I'm just exercising my liberty in Christ. Don't be critical." Well, I'm *not* being critical; I'm simply stating how God has directed me personally. I'm familiar with verses like Galatians 5:1, *"Stand fast therefore in the liberty by which Christ has made us free, and do not be entangled again with a yoke of bondage,"* and James 1:25, which refers to *"the perfect law of liberty."* But I've concluded that I *am* walking in liberty. I'm free to choose *not* to do certain things. I don't have to push the boundaries of my liberty to prove that I have moderation, and I definitely don't want my liberty to turn into license, causing other people to stumble. (See 1 Corinthians 8:9.)

Paul wrote about the dichotomy between things that were *"lawful"* for him yet were not helpful or edifying.

All things are lawful for me, but all things are not helpful. All things are lawful for me, but I will not be brought under the power of any.
(1 Corinthians 6:12)

Paul clearly recognized that some lawful activities can eventually control and enslave us.

I hope you hear my heart on this. There are various convictions or levels of consecration that God calls people to. You need to have confidence that you are walking in obedience to the Lord, glorifying Him in everything you do. (See 1 Corinthians 10:31.) Often when He takes you to a new level of influence, He will require a new level of responsibility and accountability.

Does it bother me that some Christian leaders have different standards on these kinds of issues? Not really. I've often concluded that others may, but I cannot—and that's fine with me.

Understanding the Law of Liberty

Sometimes people get the wrong idea when they read about *"the perfect law of liberty"* (James 1:25). Let me be clear about what this does *not* mean. It certainly doesn't mean that our conduct has no consequences. Nor does it mean we're in the clear if we seem to get away with something bad.

No, the perfect law of liberty means we should do the right thing even if we can get away with doing the wrong thing. Whether we're a pastor, CEO, parent, or other leader, whatever we do in private will considerably impact others. Even if nobody else sees what we are doing, when our private life is not aligned with God and His purposes, damage will be done.

One of the terrible misconceptions of our culture is that whatever we do in private is no one else's business. Yet that is faulty reasoning for three primary reasons. First, even if no one on earth realizes what we've done, God still sees and knows. Solomon pointed this out when he said, *"The eyes of the LORD are in every place, keeping watch on the evil and the good"* (Proverbs 15:3).

Second, we're all prone to self-deception, as we see in Proverbs 21:2: *"Every way of a man is right in his own eyes, but the LORD weighs the hearts."* We have a tendency to rationalize our actions and motives. Today, countless people are in danger of following the tragic example of Israel during the days of the judges, when *"everyone did what was right in his own eyes"* (Judges 21:25). That path is a sure prescription for a nation's demise.

Third, in a spiritual context, the secret sins of people in leadership will inevitably affect those under their care. God instituted parents, government officials, CEOs, and pastors as a covering of sorts. Because of this powerful principle, the decisions in a leader's personal life will always affect those under his care.

When a leader makes poor decisions, there is what I call a "breach of covering." It's like having a leaking umbrella when it rains. God has given us leaders to provide direction and protection, but if hidden sins cause holes in this spiritual umbrella, everyone underneath is bound to get wet! This means that if I'm doing something ungodly, it will open up my wife and daughter to spiritual attack. Others who look to me for leadership may also be affected, including my staff and church leaders around the world. My choices—and yours—will inevitably affect others. So never underestimate your private choices; to one degree or another, they will have public consequences.

Dr. Edwin Louis Cole used to say, "You cannot compensate by sacrifice what you've lost through disobedience." I'm surely thankful for the grace of God, because I've fallen short of His perfect standard again and again. But I continually ask Him to cleanse me of any hidden sins, for I don't want others to suffer the consequences of my wrong choices.

I've met some people in ministry who seem to think their sermons and acts of service can make up for their hidden sins. This isn't much different than the rationale of sinners who cling to the false hope that they can atone for their sins by doing good works. Dear leaders, we need to take the advice of German pastor and author Dietrich Bonhoeffer: "One act of obedience is better than one hundred sermons."

Obedience to the Lord presents unique challenges in today's world. Although our society's views of morality and political correctness are rapidly changing, God's Word never changes. If you compare yourself to the celebrities you see in the news or the people you see around you, you are using the wrong standard. Instead of trying to justify your actions by using the "everyone's doing it" excuse, I challenge you to align your life with God's unchanging Word, character, and Spirit.

Are You a Role Model?

As I mentioned earlier, a number of our professional athletes in Houston—I'm sure it's not much different in other cities—have had a reputation for visiting topless bars. One of them was asked about this several years ago, and without hesitation replied, "Hey, I've never claimed to be a role model."

Do you see the flaw in his reasoning? Whenever you accept a position of leadership or public visibility, you've set yourself up to be a role model, whether you like it or not. And if you are paid millions of dollars and are

PROVOKE-A-THOUGHT:

"THE CHURCH NEEDS HEROES TODAY. EVERY GENERATION NEEDS HEROES—MEN AND WOMEN WE CAN LOOK UP TO AND EMULATE."

constantly in the public eye, you have a responsibility to be a role model for those who follow you, especially young people.

The same is true for pastors, business leaders, teachers, and all who call themselves Christians. From the moment we say yes to our position of leadership or influence, our lives are not our own. For every new level of promotion and visibility, there must be a new level of humility, consecration, accountability, and intercession. We have a responsibility to align our attitudes and actions with the character of King Jesus and the principles of His kingdom.

If you ask people today what it takes to be a leader, you will get lots of different answers. Some may point to a certain personality type, while others may suggest it's a matter of intelligence, upbringing, or training. Yet pastor and author John MacArthur explains that the Bible presents an entirely different perspective:

> According to Scripture, virtually everything that truly qualifies a person for leadership is directly related to character. It's not about style, status, personal charisma, clout, or worldly measurements of success. Integrity is the main issue that makes the difference between a good leader and a bad one.

Another pastor and author, Chuck Swindoll, points out that the character of Christ can have a powerful impact on the people around us:

> Few things are more infectious than a godly lifestyle. The people you rub shoulders with every day need that kind of challenge. Not prudish. Not preachy. Just crackerjack clean living. Just honest-to-goodness, bone-deep, non-hypocritical integrity. Authentic obedience to God.[21]

So if you want to impact the world for Jesus, start by asking the Holy Spirit to manifest His character in your life. Your message will either be enhanced or undercut by your character.

---

21. Charles R. Swindoll, *Great Lives: David: A Man of Passion and Destiny* (Nashville, TN: Thomas Nelson, 1997), 87.

Dying to Ourselves

Commitment to integrity and godly character doesn't come easily or naturally. It involves intentionality as we pick up our Cross, follow Jesus, and die to ourselves. When it was time for Him to be rejected, mocked, beaten, and crucified, "[Jesus] *steadfastly set His face to go to Jerusalem*" (Luke 9:51). Other translations say He was "*determined*" (Luke 9:51 NASB) and "resolute" (see Luke 9:51 NIV) in His decision to press on to Jerusalem, where the Cross awaited Him. *The Message* says, "*He gathered up his courage and steeled himself for the journey to Jerusalem.*"

Take a moment to allow these words to sink in. Have you resolutely set your heart to embrace God's plan for your life, difficult and painful as it may be at times? Have you gathered up your courage and steeled yourself to fulfill His purposes for your life?

Later in the passage, we're shown a sad contrast to Jesus' determination to do the Father's will. While Jesus was the ultimate example of a person who refused to quit until He had finished His assignment, we see several fair-weather followers who made excuses for their delayed and incomplete obedience. (See Luke 51:57–62.)

The good news is that Jesus gave us a model for how we, too, can finish the race well.

> *Therefore we also, since we are surrounded by so great a cloud of witnesses, let us **lay aside every weight**, and the **sin** which so easily ensnares us, and let us **run with endurance the race that is set before us**, **looking unto Jesus**, the author and finisher of our faith, who for the **joy that was set before Him endured the cross**, despising the shame, and has sat down at the right hand of the throne of God. For consider Him who endured such hostility from sinners against Himself, **lest you become weary and discouraged in your souls.*** (Hebrews 12:1–3)

This passage shows how we can walk in perseverance and victory. We must lay aside our encumbrances, sins, and snares. Instead of dwelling on our difficult circumstances or listening to our critics, we must fix our eyes on Jesus. Like Him, we must look beyond our present situation to the joy set before us.

If we do these things, we will avoid becoming *"weary and discouraged."* As Jesus declared at the end of His mission, we can one day say as we complete *our* assigned purpose, *"It is finished!"* (John 19:30).

Victory via Brokenness

If I asked you whether you're a broken person, you might not know how to answer. On the one hand, we're all broken in that we've been damaged by the fall in Genesis 3. Ever since that fateful occasion when Adam and Eve disobeyed God's command, we all have sinned and fallen short of the glory of God. (See Romans 3:23.) And, as a result, we're scarred and damaged, in need of forgiveness and restoration.

But that's not the kind of brokenness I'm referring to. There's another kind of brokenness that's not only positive but essential for those who want to be greatly used by God. This brokenness is found often throughout the Bible; here are a few examples:

The sacrifices of God are a broken spirit, a broken and a contrite heart—these, O God, You will not despise. (Psalm 51:17)

The Lord is near to those who have a broken heart, and saves such as have a contrite spirit. (Psalm 34:18)

"Heaven is my throne, and the earth is my footstool. Where is the house you will build for me? Where will my resting place be? Has not my hand made all these things, and so they came into being?" declares the Lord. "These are the ones I look on with favor: those who are humble and contrite in spirit, and who tremble at my word." (Isaiah 66:1–2 NIV)

God is very clear about those He will *"look on with favor."* As Christian leaders, we should want to be in that category!

Notice that the only pathway to this kind of divine favor is through humility, contrition, and brokenness before the Lord. He's the "Stone" we must intentionally cast ourselves upon to find this kind of brokenness, for He says, *"Whoever falls on this stone will be broken; but on whomever it falls, it will grind him to powder"* (Matthew 21:44). In other words, we must humble ourselves or run the risk of being humbled by God's judgment. *"Everyone who exalts himself will be humbled, and he who humbles himself will be exalted"* (Luke 18:14).

> **PROVOKE-A-THOUGHT:**
>
> "SUCCESS IS NOT NECESSARILY GAINED DUE TO ONE'S *ABILITY AND APTITUDE,* BUT MORE TO DO WITH ONE'S *AVAILABILITY AND ATTITUDE.* SHOW UP; BE AVAILABLE, AND KEEP A RIGHT ATTITUDE."

The humility and brokenness I'm talking about is not a matter of masochism or self-abasement. Far from it. It doesn't mean beating ourselves up but rather seeing ourselves in light of the awesome majesty of our Creator. We realize that we're not meant to be self-made people, able to achieve our own success apart from God. Instead, we realize the truth of the psalmist's words *"It is He who has made us, and not we ourselves"* (Psalm 100:3).

Why This Waste?

Why does God value brokenness so much? Perhaps the answer is best illustrated in this beautiful experience in the life of Jesus:

> *While he was in Bethany, reclining at the table in the home of Simon the Leper, a woman came with an alabaster jar of very expensive perfume, made of pure nard.* **She broke the jar and poured the perfume on his head.** *Some of those present were saying indignantly to one another,* **"Why this waste** *of perfume? It could have been sold for* **more than a year's wages** *and the money given to the poor." And they re-*

buked her harshly. "Leave her alone," said Jesus. "Why are you bother-
ing her? She has done a beautiful thing to me. The poor you will always
have with you, and you can help them any time you want. But you will
not always have me. She did what she could. She poured perfume on my
body beforehand to prepare for my burial. Truly I tell you, **wherever**
the gospel is preached throughout the world, what she has done will
also be told, in memory of her."   (Mark 14:3–9 NIV)

Let's begin by looking at the *end* of the story. Jesus said that this woman's lavish act of worship was so significant that it would continue to be told
"wherever the gospel is preached throughout the world." Why do you think He
said this? The key, I believe, is the woman's passionate love for Jesus—the
fuel that should motivate everything we do as Christian leaders.

The woman's passion led to *extreme generosity.* In one relatively brief act
of worship, she invested *"more than a year's wages."* Wow. I don't know how
much your income is in a year, but can you imagine pouring it out on Jesus
in a single evening?

But none of this would have been possible without brokenness. You
see, the *"very expensive perfume, made of pure nard"* was locked away in an
alabaster jar. The incredible fragrance wasn't released until she had *broken*
the jar. That's why God puts such a high value on our brokenness. He has
put the sweet fragrance of Jesus in our spirit, but it is unleashed only to the
extent that we are broken before the Lord.

There's a beautiful footnote found in the parallel account in John 12:1–
8. Verse 3 says, *"The house was filled with the fragrance of the oil."* The woman
wasn't focused on spreading fragrance throughout the entire house. Her
focus was solely on anointing Jesus, the One she loved. Yet the result went
beyond just Jesus Himself—the fragrance was carried throughout the
whole house, as well as throughout the world.

In the same way, when we're broken before the Lord, the fragrance
of our worship will fill our homes, our churches, and our communities.
(See 2 Corinthians 2:14.) No wonder Jesus said that this woman's powerful
story would accompany the gospel to the four corners of the earth.

21

Deadly Sins on the Way to Your Promised Land

An entire generation of Israelites failed to enter into the Promised Land. After a thrilling supernatural exit from Egypt and crossing of the Red Sea, the Israelites still didn't finish their race well. Why? The writer of Hebrews says they missed out on entering God's rest—their purpose and destiny—because of unbelief and disobedience. (See Hebrews 3:18–19; 4:11.)

In addition, in 1 Corinthians, we're given more details of how the Israelites got off track. During their desert wanders, they engaged in five specific sins that brought God's judgment and kept them from enjoying His full blessings.

*With most of them God was not well pleased, for their bodies were scattered in the wilderness. Now these things became our examples, to the intent that we should not **lust** after evil things as they also lusted. And do not become **idolaters** as were some of them. As it is written, "The people sat down to eat and drink, and rose up to play." Nor let us commit **sexual immorality**, as some of them did, and in one day twenty-three thousand fell; nor let us **tempt Christ**, as some of them also tempted, and were destroyed by serpents; nor **complain**, as some of them also complained, and were destroyed by the destroyer. Now all these things happened to them as examples, and they were written for* *our admonition, upon whom the ends of the ages have come. Therefore let him who thinks he stands take heed lest he fall.*

(1 Corinthians 10:5–12)

Let's look at the sins described by Paul in this passage:

1. Lust

2. Idolatry

3. Sexual immorality

4. Tempting the Lord

5. Complaining (grumbling)

Paul lists these five sins of the Israelites not just as a history lesson. They are warnings for us Christians today, *"upon whom the ends of the ages have come"* (1 Corinthians 10:11). In our culture, each of these sins runs rampant. The majority of the ads on TV and in secular magazines are designed to tempt us to lust, idolatry, or sexual immorality. Young people come to me all the time, confiding about their struggles in these areas. "Doug, I'm bound by pornography; the lust of the flesh is controlling my life," many of them say.

There are also a large number of professing Christians who provoke God's judgment with their cavalier attitude toward the sins in their lives. This is what we mean by "tempting Christ." They've accepted the misguided notion that, with God's grace, they will never face any consequences for unconfessed sins. But the Bible says quite the contrary:

If we sin willfully after we have received the knowledge of the truth, there no longer remains a sacrifice for sins, but a certain fearful expectation of judgment. (Hebrews 10:26–27)

Yes, you are saved by grace, my friend; but sin is nothing to play around with. If there are hidden sins in your life, I encourage you to take a moment right now to ask God to forgive you, cleanse you, and restore you. Don't delay! Now is the time to put an axe to the roots of any sins you've been harboring.

I've met many people who make excuses for their sins and addictions. They say they are someone else's fault, like their parents or their spouse. Or they use the "I'm only human" cop-out. I've heard all the excuses, and some of them I've used myself. But in this same passage, Paul cuts off every excuse:

> No temptation has overtaken you except such as is common to man; but God is faithful, who will not allow you to be tempted beyond what you are able, but with the temptation will also make the way of escape, that you may be able to bear it.   (1 Corinthians 10:13)

Look at the highlights of this powerful verse:

+ When you face temptations, you need to recognize that you're not alone. The same temptations are *"common to man,"* from Bible times all the way until today.

+ Your hope for victory over temptation must rest on *"God [who] is faithful."* You will not overcome the enemy in *your* strength but in *His* strength.

+ For every temptation you face, God has already provided a *"way of escape."* You can't make the flimsy excuse, "The devil made me do it," because God offers you a solution.

+ Your temptation may seem unbearable at the moment, but this verse promises that with God's help, you will *"be able to bear it."*

Do you see what good news this is? If you are struggling with temptation today, the Lord wants to help you find victory. And when Jesus sets you free from it, you will be *"free indeed"* (John 8:36).

The Sin of Grumbling

I've purposefully saved the sins of grumbling and idolatry to discuss last. Some of the other sins are more obvious and apparent, but often these two are largely a matter of the heart. Although these two sins are quite common and very grievous in the eyes of God, rarely are they mentioned in a sermon or discussed in an accountability group.

Many Christian leaders are proud to say they have never succumbed to any big sins, such as sexual immorality. Yet they sure do grumble a lot, and many of them also gossip—another one of the more acceptable Christian sins. Murmuring and gossip are such a serious problem that I sometimes wonder if they have destroyed more individuals, marriages, churches, and careers than sexual immorality.

Grumbling is like a spiritual and emotional cancer, replicating and growing until all life is gone. It's the very opposite of positive attributes like gratitude, contentment, and thankfulness. The Bible repeatedly tells us that gratitude attracts God's blessings, while grumbling attracts adversity. Many of the trials the Israelites experienced in the wilderness were the direct result of their ungrateful attitude and grumbling against Moses and against the Lord.

The apostle Paul took up this theme in his letter to the Philippians:

Do all things without complaining and disputing, that you may become blameless and harmless, children of God without fault in the midst of a crooked and perverse generation, among whom you shine as lights in the world, holding fast the word of life, so that I may rejoice in the day of Christ that I have not run in vain or labored in vain.
(Philippians 2:14–16)

PROVOKE-A-THOUGHT:

"PRIVATE POSTURE AFFECTS PUBLIC POSITION. PRIVATE CHOICES HAVE PUBLIC CONSEQUENCES."

This is a pretty challenging word of instruction, isn't it? No complaining at all? That's a pretty high standard. Yet Paul paints a breathtaking picture of what happens when we do things without grumbling. We will become *"blameless and harmless, children of God without fault in the midst of a crooked and perverse generation."*

You see, few qualities will make us stand out from the crowd like gratitude. In a culture of entitlement and complaining, we can make an incredible impact. Paul says that gratitude will enable us to *"shine as lights in the world,"* and that we also will be able to powerfully share the *"word of life"* with others.

What About Idolatry?

When you talk with most Christians about idolatry, they picture an idol like the golden calf the Israelites worshiped at the foot of Mount Sinai. (See Exodus 32.) "Oh, I would never do anything like that!" they say in disgust.

I'm convinced that idolatry is much more pervasive than we think, not only in our society, but even in the church. We might not have any golden calves, but we find plenty of other things to worship: celebrities, wealth, youth, pleasure, sex, food, sports, clothes, cars, houses, smartphones, computers, alcohol, and drugs—and the list goes on.

What is idolatry? It's not just worshiping some kind of gold or silver object. Idolatry is anything that masters our affections more than Jesus. This means that even our spouses and kids can be idols in our lives. Our careers or ministries can be idols, as well as success.

Idolatry isn't something that affects just unbelievers. John was writing to Christians when he warned:

> Do not love the world or the things in the world. If anyone loves the world, the love of the Father is not in him. For all that is in the world—the lust of the flesh, the lust of the eyes, and the pride of life—is not of the Father but is of the world. And the world is passing away, and the lust of it; but he who does the will of God abides forever.
> (1 John 2:15–17)

Take a moment and allow the Holy Spirit to search your heart right now. Ask Him to reveal any idols you've been harboring, anything that has diverted your affection away from Jesus. Then ask the Lord to restore you to passionate, wholehearted devotion to Him above all else. (See 2 Corinthians 11:2–3.)

PROVOKE-A-THOUGHT:

"AS A SOCIETY (AND SADLY EVEN IN THE CHURCH) WE ARE WITNESSING THE HUMAN INCLINATION TO CASUALLY DISREGARD WHAT PREVIOUS GENERATIONS HAVE HELD TO BE OF FUNDAMENTAL IMPORTANCE. WE HAVE BECOME MORE AND MORE ENAMORED WITH CELEBRITY, SUCCESS, AND POWER. THE LUST OF THE EYE, LUST OF THE FLESH, AND THE PRIDE OF LIFE. LUST AND PRIDE, ALL ROOTED IN SELF—SELF-ABSORPTION, SELF-CENTEREDNESS, SELF-ADULATION, SELF-RIGHTEOUSNESS. SELFISHNESS!"

What Would You Rather Have?

For over fifty years, George Beverly Shea sang a wonderful old hymn by Rhea F. Miller at Billy Graham's evangelistic crusades:

"I'd Rather Have Jesus"
I'd rather have Jesus than silver or gold;
I'd rather be His than have riches untold;
I'd rather have Jesus than houses or land;
I'd rather be led by His nail-pierced hand.

Than to be the king of a vast domain
And be held in sin's dread sway.
I'd rather have Jesus than anything
This world affords today.

I'd rather have Jesus than men's applause;
I'd rather be faithful to His dear cause;
I'd rather have Jesus than worldwide fame;
I'd rather be true to His holy name.[22]

22. Rhea F. Miller, "I'd Rather Have Jesus," 1922.

This song is about the choice we each must make. Will we choose Jesus or idolatry? Will we choose Him or money, material possessions, and power? Will we cling to Him or chase people's applause and the fleeting fame of this world?

The first book of John ends with a sobering warning for every Christian, and especially for those of us called to leadership: *"Little children, guard yourselves from idols"* (1 John 5:21). This is important, timely advice for leaders who want to faithfully run the race and finish well.

Possessing the Promised Land

I love the account in Numbers 13 about the twelve spies sent to investigate the Promised Land. God has ordained a wonderful Promised Land for you and me as well, but we will face some of the same obstacles as the Israelites.

Ten of the spies acknowledged that it was a great land. *"It truly flows with milk and honey, and this is its fruit"* (Numbers 13:27), they said. However, the fears of these ten spies overcame their faith. *"Nevertheless the people who dwell in the land are strong; the cities are fortified and very large; moreover we saw the descendants of Anak [giants] there"* (Numbers 13:28).

However, two of the spies, Caleb and Joshua, came back with a positive report. Caleb urged, *"Let us go up at once and take possession, for we are well able to overcome it"* (Numbers 13:30).

Sadly, fear prevailed, and the people believed the ten spies rather than Caleb and Joshua. They adopted the message of unbelief and ended up with a dismal view of themselves: *"We were like grasshoppers in our own sight, and so we were in their sight"* (Numbers 13:33).

It's easy to look upon the ten fearful, unbelieving spies with disdain, but we all battle the same temptation. Will we choose faith or fear? Will we believe God and boldly possess our Promised Land, or will we cower in timidity? Will we see the overwhelming greatness of the Lord, or find ourselves overwhelmed by "giants" and difficult circumstances that make us feel like grasshoppers?

One of the most important traits of leaders who finish well is that they choose to face their giants in the name of the Lord. Even amid the challenges of life and leadership, they consistently maintain a vision of their destination—a land of hope, promise, and fruitfulness.

You see, Caleb and Joshua had a different attitude and spirit than the other spies. They reasoned that if God had given the Israelites this fantastic land flowing with milk and honey, then it didn't matter how big the giants or obstacles were. After all, their God was *bigger*! Even before the apostle Paul wrote the book of Romans, these men of faith instinctively knew, "*If God is for us, who can be against us?*" (Romans 8:31).

As Winkie Pratney pointed out, God allowed the Israelites to journey through the wilderness in order to set them free from their mind-set in Egypt, where they had lived in fear, bondage, and slavery. Sometimes, we have to go through difficult times and challenges in order to find out what we're really made of. God won't let us go through these trials unless He believes we can handle them. (See 1 Corinthians 10:13.) He has a divine calling for each of us, and He's more than able to help us face our "giants" and fulfill His destiny for our lives.

Confronting the Status Quo

One of the biggest giants leaders face is getting stuck in the status quo. Salvation Army cofounder Catherine Booth rightly observed, "If we are to better the future we must disturb the present."[23] Throughout the Bible, God raised leaders to disturb the way things were done in order to create a better future.

Think about how Jesus interacted with the religious leaders of His day. The leaders, and pretty much all the Jews, eagerly anticipated the coming Messiah; but they envisioned a Messiah that was going to come and free them from domination by the Romans, not free them from sin and death.

When Jesus the Messiah came on the scene, He didn't fit into the boxes people had created for Him. Instead of spending any time confronting the

---

23. Catherine Booth quoted in Frederick St. George de Latour Booth-Tucker, *The Life of Catherine Booth: The Mother of the Salvation Army*, vol. 2 (London: Revell, 1892), 425.

Romans, He confronted the status quo in the temple and the synagogues! No wonder He attracted enemies among the religious leaders. The status quo always fights back.

I've seen countless men and women begin their ministry or career with high hopes of bringing transformation and making a difference. But after years of frustration and banging their heads against the wall, they've concluded that change just isn't possible. They tell me something like, "Doug, I fought the system, and the system won."

Let me make a few observations about all this. First, if you are truly functioning as a transformational leader, you *will* face opposition at times. You're swimming upstream, after all. As the saying goes, "If everything is going your way, you're probably headed in the wrong direction!" So don't be discouraged if change comes much slower than you hoped. I am well aware that *"hope deferred makes the heart sick"* (Proverbs 13:12), but that verse concludes with a great promise: *"When the desire comes, it is a tree of life."*

Second, if you're a visionary, you shouldn't be surprised if it takes a while for others to catch up with your vision. You've been called to boldly march ahead of the pack—and you will need both patience and persistence to be the change agent God wants you to be.

22

Seizing Your Opportunity

When many Christians look at today's world or their prospects for the future, all they see is doom and gloom. And indeed, we live in a world full of crises. However, to live triumphantly in such times, we must have God's perspective, which certainly isn't negative.

> *Arise, shine; for your light has come! And the glory of the LORD is risen upon you. For behold, the darkness shall cover the earth, and deep darkness the people; but the LORD will arise over you, and His glory will be seen upon you. The Gentiles shall come to your light, and kings to the brightness of your rising. "Lift up your eyes all around, and see: They all gather together, they come to you; your sons shall come from afar, and your daughters shall be nursed at your side. Then you shall see and become radiant, and your heart shall swell with joy."*
> (Isaiah 60:1–5)

This describes our present situation so well, doesn't it? Yes, there is great darkness covering much of the earth, but this is no time to despair. God tells us to rise and shine! He is shining His light upon every hungry heart, and is using us to reveal His glory to a lost and dying world. Rather than sinking into despair, we need to seize our opportunities to impact the world for Christ!

I love the statement made by economist Paul Romer several years ago: "A crisis is a terrible thing to waste." Yes, we live in a world of crises, but this presents us with opportunities we must not waste. Filled with the Spirit of God, we are called to be the light of the world (see Matthew 5:14–16), and light always shines brightest during the darkest hours.

Amid His description of the terrible crises that will come upon the earth in the end times, Jesus makes a wonderful statement. There will be false prophets, wars, commotions, earthquakes, plagues, and famines. They will indeed be perilous times, and we're already experiencing the birth pangs He predicted. However, tucked away in this bleak picture is a fantastic ray of hope. These difficult times, Jesus said, *"will lead to an opportunity for your testimony"* (Luke 21:13 NASB).

Who is the Lord talking to here? This is a message of encouragement for the believers who live during the end times. Instead of being discouraged and defeated by the traumas around us, we are called to seize the opportunity to be bold witnesses for Jesus! He will prepare and position us to bring heaven's healing balm to everyone affected by the chaos. As the darkness grows, so the light of the gospel will shine brighter in our lives.

However, there's an urgency in this hour. As Jesus said, *"I must work the works of Him who sent Me while it is day; the night is coming when no one can work"* (John 9:4). And although we're entering a period of unparalleled opportunities, Leonard Ravenhill was correct when he said, "The opportunity of a lifetime needs to be seized during the lifetime of the opportunity."

Likewise, the apostle Paul underscored our urgent need to seize the opportunities before us:

> *Make the most of every opportunity in these evil days. Don't act thoughtlessly, but understand what the Lord wants you to do.*
> (Ephesians 5:16–17 NLT)

The Greek word translated *"opportunity"* here is *kairos*. If ever there was a "kairos" moment in human history, it is now! What does that mean for you and me? Paul emphatically says that it's time to *"understand what the Lord wants you to do."*

Ready to Go Home?

I meet many Christians who can't wait for Jesus to swoop down and take them home to heaven. On one hand, I certainly understand this. The Bible says we should be living in anticipation of Jesus' return. As the apostle John wrote in Revelation 22:20, the cry of our heart should be, *"Even so, come, Lord Jesus!"*

But there's a balance to everything. In *The Wizard of Oz*, Dorothy kept clicking her heels, saying, "There's no place like home. There's no place like home." Many Christians are very much like this, and it's commendable that they recognize their citizenship in heaven. (See Philippians 3:20.) However, we're called to make a *difference* in this world, so we must be active, not just wait around for Jesus to rescue us. Yes, He will soon return, but until then, He's commanded us, *"Occupy till I come"* (Luke 19:13 KJV).

So instead of clicking our heels and saying, "There's no place like home," our cry today should be, "My life is not my own. My life is not my own." You see, it's not about you and me, it's about Him. And rather than putting our focus on maximizing our safety and security, our heart should be set on fulfilling His purposes right up until our final breath.

And what, exactly, is God's central purpose for us during this earthly life? The Bible describes a wide variety of different ministries that He calls individuals to, but Paul made it clear that each one of us is called to *"the ministry of reconciliation"*:

> *Now all things are of God, who has reconciled us to Himself through Jesus Christ, and has given us the ministry of reconciliation, that is, that God was in Christ reconciling the world to Himself, not imputing their trespasses to them, and has committed to us the word of reconciliation. Now then, we are ambassadors for Christ, as though God were pleading through us: we implore you on Christ's behalf, be reconciled to God.* (2 Corinthians 5:18–20)

You may be a pastor, called to preach and teach the Word behind a pulpit, but that's not Paul's focus here. The lost and needy people we are called to reach are seldom sitting in the pews of our churches. Instead, they are out in the streets, in the bars, or living beside us in our neighborhoods. In the midst of their difficult, chaotic, and disappointing lives, they need people of God to reach out to them as peacemakers and ministers of reconciliation. We're called to be ambassadors of Christ to bring peace amid life's storms. (See 2 Corinthians 5:20.)

In addition to bringing peace and reconciliation to people's lives, we're called to be witnesses of God, revealing what He has shown us and done for us in our lives. When Peter and John were commanded not to speak or teach in the name of Jesus, they replied, *"We cannot but speak the things which we have seen and heard"* (Acts 4:20).

What have you *"seen and heard"*? Are you applying those truths to your life in practical ways? Are you passing those truths on to the coming generation? These questions don't just apply to some elite group of professional leaders. They apply to all people, regardless of vocation or area of leadership and influence God has called them to.

Businesspeople Who Care

"Tonight, I choose kindness and will be kind to the poor, for they are alone. Kind to the rich, for they are afraid."

Tan Sri Francis Yeoh spoke the words above at a speech delivered to an audience of fifty thousand people at the 2003 YTL Concert of Celebration, held on the lawn of the Royal Crescent in Bath, England, an event that featured The Three Tenors, The Royal Philharmonic Orchestra, the Bath Camerata choir, and the Choristers of Bath Abbey. Concert tickets were free, but contributions for charities were collected from many of the guests.

In his address, Yeoh honored heroes of the faith who helped to shape the spiritual culture of Bath, including George Whitfield and John Wesley. One of the honored guests was Lady Cope, a descendent of Horatio G. Spafford, the author of Dr. Yeoh's favorite hymn, "It Is Well with My Soul." At Yeoh's request, the hymn was performed by The Three Tenors.

Christians—not just pastors but laymen in business, engineering, high tech, medicine—need to be at the forefront of solving the world's problems. But it is going to take vision and leadership to get it done.

"If we tackle the root causes of injustice and deprivation," Yeoh insists, "we will create a better life for all. We need to renew our faith in that Great Engineer—the Creator of the universe, our Lord God."

True Witnesses

Before ascending into heaven, Jesus said that His followers would receive the Holy Spirit, empowering them to be His witnesses.

> *But you shall receive power when the Holy Spirit has come upon you; and you shall be witnesses to Me in Jerusalem, and in all Judea and Samaria, and to the end of the earth.* (Acts 1:8)

The Greek word translated *"witnesses"* is *martys*, from which we get the word *martyrs*. What a stunning reminder of the gravity of our call to lay our lives down to be witnesses for Christ.

Of course, not all witnesses are *true* witnesses. Right in the midst of the Ten Commandments, we're told, *"You shall not bear false witness against your neighbor"* (Exodus 20:16). And if it's terrible to bear false witness against your neighbor, think of how weighty it is to bear false witness against the Son of God! Yet that's what happens every time we reflect attitudes or lifestyles that misrepresent the character of our Lord.

So what does a true witness look like? First of all, a true witness is committed to reflecting the image and likeness of Christ in his life. (See Genesis 1:26–27; Romans 8:29.) Although this doesn't require perfection by any means, our lives should look much different from the unbelieving world around us.

Various translations of Proverbs 14:25 say that a true witness *"saves lives"* (NIV), *"rescues lives"* (HCSB), and *"delivers souls"* (NKJV). Let that statement sink in for a moment. If you're a true witness for Christ, an important part of your life will be to rescue people from desperate situations and eternal destruction. You will want to be a tangible expression of Christ, an ambassador of His hope and healing to people who are shipwrecked.

Radical but Balanced

If the devil can't lull us to sleep or make us lukewarm, he will try to make us unbalanced in some area of our lives. Sometimes, Christians are knocked off balance even when they seem super spiritual, claiming to be serving God while neglecting clear biblical mandates. (See Mark 7:9–13.)

We need to remember Solomon's wisdom about keeping the proper balance: *"A false balance is an abomination to the* Lord, *but a just weight is his delight"* (Proverbs 11:1 esv). For example, in radical devotion to the Lord, we shouldn't neglect the proper care of our bodies. God made us *"spirit and soul and body"* (1 Thessalonians 5:23), and each of these facets of our life is important to maintain.

I had the privilege of contributing to *The Maximized Living Bible*, in which I wrote, "Sluggish minds live in sluggish bodies." In other words, we shouldn't be so spiritual and heavenly minded that we abuse or neglect our physical bodies, which comprise the temple of the Holy Spirit. (See 1 Corinthians 6:19–20.)

Sometimes the most spiritual thing you can do as a leader is get some rest. Jesus often went off by Himself to the mountain to rest and pray (see Matthew 14:23), and He gave that same advice to His disciples: *"Come aside by yourselves to a deserted place and rest a while"* (Mark 6:31). There are times when you just need to shut things down. Turn off your computer and mute your cell phone. Eliminate as much noise as possible, and focus again on receiving the Lord's love and hearing His gentle whisper.

Many years ago, I learned from Ray Comfort and Winkie Pratney the importance of following God's command to take a day off

PROVOKE-A-THOUGHT:

"CHOICES HAVE CONSEQUENCES, REGARDLESS OF HOW MUCH WE TRY TO JUSTIFY, EXCUSE, OR EVEN TRY TO LEGALIZE THEM."

each week to rest, or a Sabbath day. If you're a pastor, you need to find one day each week to stop working and disengage from any unnecessary activities. This is a vital time not only to get physical rest but also to renew your emotions, rest your mind, and improve your mental health. Rather than being a matter of legalism, the Sabbath principle is for our *benefit*. As Jesus said, *"The Sabbath was made for man, and not man for the Sabbath"* (Mark 2:27).

Remember, you aren't *just* a spiritual being. The Bible teaches that you are spirit, soul, and body, and He wants all of these components in alignment, because you are His holy temple.

23

God's Gold Medalists

Japanese gymnast Shun Fujimoto was favored to win the gold medal during the 1976 Summer Olympics in Montreal, Canada. During the floor exercises, he broke a kneecap but still managed to score 9.5 on the pommel horse and 9.7 on the rings. Somehow, after dismounting from the rings eight feet above ground, he landed perfectly on his feet. Afterward, he raised his arms in victory and then buckled to the ground in excruciating pain. The force of the impact dislocated Fujimoto's knee and tore ligaments. Doctors couldn't figure out how he completed his routine with such great success.[24]

With rugged determination and perseverance, Fujimoto helped his team edge out the Soviet Union for the gold medal. When asked how he did it, Fujimoto replied, "My desire to win was greater than my moment of pain."

This unwavering desire is vital to our success as leaders. Undoubtedly there will be moments of pain during our journey on the leadership highway. In order to finish well, we must have unflagging passion to reach our destination. An eternal *"gold medal"* is at stake.

You've all been to the stadium and seen the athletes race. Everyone runs; one wins. Run to win. All good athletes train hard. They do it for a gold medal that tarnishes and fades. You're after one that's gold eternally. (1 Corinthians 9:24–25 MSG)

---

24. "Shun Fujimoto," https://en.wikipedia.org/wiki/Shun_Fujimoto.

Yes, despite Shun Fujimoto's amazing accomplishment, he won a gold medal that will tarnish and fade. But if we press through adversity and finish well, God will offer us a prize that is *"gold eternally," "an imperishable crown"* (1 Corinthians 9:25 NKJV).

<table>
<tr><td>

PROVOKE-A-THOUGHT:

"OUR DESIRE TO WIN MUST BE GREATER THAN OUR MOMENTS OF STRUGGLE OR PAIN."

</td><td>

Every Christian leader I've ever met has hit a wall at some point in their lives. "What in the world am I doing?" we ask ourselves. "Maybe I should do something different with my life."

At that moment when we're tempted to quit, it's more important than ever to take courage and fix our

</td></tr>
</table>

eyes on Jesus. (See Hebrews 12:1–3.) During tough times, your leadership is needed more than ever. Even though we are bound to see some dark days along the way, I'm confident we've been called *"for such a time as this"* (Esther 4:14).

Winning Our M-E-D-A-L

I want to share with you the acronym MEDAL, which has helped me focus on kingdom principles.

M – Message

From time to time, we each must ask ourselves whether the message we teach and the message we live are aligned with the values of the kingdom. Everything we do should be filtered through the lens of God's Word. In order to be the Lord's messengers, we must continually ensure that our message lines up with His. And if we've truly received a message from God, it will be *clear*, not wavering or vacillating. (See 1 Corinthians 14:8; 2 Corinthians 1:17–20.)

E – Evangelism

Paul told his spiritual son Timothy, *"Do the work of an evangelist, fulfill your ministry"* (2 Timothy 4:5). In a practical sense, this means expanding

God's kingdom by sharing the good news of the gospel with others. Some preachers seem to excel in sharing bad news, beating people up rather than providing the hope and transformation offered in the gospel of Christ. Furthermore, in order to be authentic, the good news of our message should reflect the good news of Christ's message in our lives. People will be drawn to the Lord when they see what He is doing in our lives.

In my early days of ministry, we used to preach on the streets and do outreaches at big events. We would make a big splash by carrying Crosses and using bull horns to loudly proclaim our message. You've probably seen other preachers use this approach on street corners, at parades, or on college campuses. They typically carry a big black Bible, and scream at the top of their lungs, "Repent, you evildoers!"

Well, what is the fruit of that kind of evangelism? All I can say is that I've found it much more effective to reach out to people with *compassion* and engage them in *conversation* with the objective of engaging their hearts. Some believers seem to think that effective evangelism is primarily a matter of winning arguments, when it's really about winning people's *hearts*.

D – Discipleship

In order to grow in the Lord and properly develop as Christian leaders, we must be discipled and mentored, but the process doesn't stop there. We must raise up others to become fully devoted followers of Christ.

Discipleship is frequently misunderstood. It means much more than just reading a few books and sitting in church services, seminars, and lecture halls. While there's nothing wrong with such things, they don't get to the heart of true discipleship. Paul explained this distinction quite clearly to the Corinthians:

I do not write these things to shame you, but as my beloved children I warn you. For though you might have ten thousand instructors in Christ, yet you do not have many fathers; for in Christ Jesus I have begotten you through the gospel. Therefore I urge you, imitate me.
(1 Corinthians 4:14–16)

You see, Paul was not just a Bible teacher or instructor to the Christians in Corinth. He had a relationship with them—he saw them as his *"beloved children."* But sadly, Paul reported that there weren't many spiritual fathers and mothers in the church—a shortage we still have in the present day. As a result, many believers don't have spiritual mentors to show them godly examples and hold them accountable.

PROVOKE-A-THOUGHT:

"CHAMPIONS ARE NOT HINDERED BY OBSTACLES, BUT DETERMINE TO OVERCOME THEM."

Why do we all need mentors—spiritual fathers and mothers—to disciple us as followers of Jesus? One important reason is that discipleship is a process, not a onetime event. I call those who undergo discipleship "disciples in training," or DITs. You see, Christian growth is meant to be a lifelong process. We're never supposed to reach some comfortable spiritual plateau and just rest on our laurels. Day by day, converts should grow as disciples, ambassadors, and, ultimately, leaders.

The writer of the book of Hebrews speaks about the serious problem of believers who never really grow up, which is still a problem today.

Though by this time you ought to be teachers, you need someone to teach you the elementary truths of God's word all over again. You need milk, not solid food! Anyone who lives on milk, being still an infant, is not acquainted with the teaching about righteousness. But solid food is for the mature, who by constant use have trained themselves to distinguish good from evil. (Hebrews 5:12–14 NIV)

Instead of growing into mature Christians, able to teach others, many people are still spiritual infants. Although they've heard countless sermons and read numerous inspirational books, they still aren't ready to eat *"solid food"* or help others become fully devoted followers of Jesus.

I've been extremely blessed over the years to have had some true men of God mentor me, people like Leonard Ravenhill, David Wilkerson, Edwin Louis Cole, and several others. I didn't always have a lot of time with these men, but they profoundly influenced me in the brief snippets of time we had together.

For example, I met Leonard Ravenhill fairly late in his life, yet he cared for me and adopted me as a spiritual son. I could be traveling anywhere in the world, and when I called him, he would answer and say, "Hi, brother Doug. I was just praying for you." That was always such an encouragement to me.

Brother Ravenhill loved me, I was sure of that. But in addition to encouragement, sometimes he dished out tough love. I'll never forget the time he pointed his long, bony finger in my face and said, "You're more ignorant than I thought!" I immediately melted under conviction from the Holy Spirit, crying out for mercy, "Oh, God, please help me. I've fallen short in so many ways."

When I met Edwin Louis Cole, I was a complete nobody, but he proudly introduced me to others as his Japanese son. He recruited me to help him with the National Men's Conference in 1984 and also included me in many other events he sponsored. Neither Dr. Cole nor any of my other mentors was perfect, yet their message left an indelible impression on my life.

I remember driving with Dr. Cole one day after a meeting in which he boldly called me to get right with God. He leaned out the window of a blue van and cried out to God with tears in his eyes, "Lord, would You give me a little more time to reach more men and save more families?" On another occasion, he called me and some other men up to his hotel room for a spontaneous prayer meeting. We knelt on pillows on the floor and sought God.

Experiences like these have had a lasting impact on my life. These men were always learning and growing in their intimacy with the Lord. They were true disciples, ambassadors, and leaders. And even as they eagerly taught others, they also were eager to learn anything they could from them. Why? Because they knew that they, too, were disciples in training.

I'm always wary of Christian leaders who act as if they've arrived. Personally, the only time I can say I've arrived is when the GPS on my rental car says, "You've arrived at your destination." I know that my journey toward maturity is ongoing and that I still have a long way to go before reaching perfection.

The mighty apostle Paul spoke of his ongoing quest for greater maturity.

> *Not that I have already attained, or am already perfected; but I press on, that I may lay hold of that for which Christ Jesus has also laid hold of me. Brethren, I do not count myself to have apprehended; but one thing I do, forgetting those things which are behind and reaching forward to those things which are ahead, I press toward the goal for the prize of the upward call of God in Christ Jesus. Therefore let us, as many as are mature, have this mind; and if in anything you think otherwise, God will reveal even this to you. Nevertheless, to the degree that we have already attained, let us walk by the same rule, let us be of the same mind.* (Philippians 3:12–16)

First, Paul gives a powerful disclaimer about his own life. Despite his incredible accomplishments, he knew he hadn't arrived at perfection by any means. In fact, he was still devoting himself to pressing on *"toward the goal for the prize of the upward call of God in Christ Jesus."* I love that God's call for each of is always *"upward,"* meaning we still have lots of room for growth!

After sharing his quest for more of Christ, Paul shifts his attention to everyone else who claims to be mature. He challenges them to have the same mind-set as him—seeing themselves as disciples in training, not people who have already arrived at the ultimate level of spiritual development.

A – Ambassador

The process of discipleship doesn't end when converts become good church members, able to sing a few worship choruses and quote a few Bible verses. Ultimately, disciples are meant to grow into ambassadors, representing Christ wherever they go. This goes far beyond Sunday-morning

Christianity, and involves taking the kingdom of God into every area of life.

One of my daily prayers is, "Lord, help me to be an ambassador for You in everything I think, say, and do today. Help me to bring glory and honor to Your name as a faithful ambassador." My identity as an ambassador of Christ is incredibly important to me, as it should be to you. At times, when people ask me what I do, I reply, "I'm an ambassador!"

What does this mean on a practical level? Wherever God sends me, I understand that I'm not there representing my kingdom but rather His kingdom. It's not about me—or about you. We're simply called to enter the various areas of our culture as ambassadors for the greatest Leader of all time, King Jesus. When we recognize that we're operating under His authority to glorify His name, we can cast aside our fears and insecurities, knowing that He will back us up on our mission.

God has sent me as His representative to the offices of governors, mayors, and police chiefs. At times, I've been His ambassador to professional athletes, community leaders, and celebrities. And I've also been privileged to meet with the presidents of several countries. Was I intimidated by these opportunities? Not really. As Ezra Taft Benson wisely observed, "He who kneels before God can stand before anyone." If we've spent time in the presence of the King of the universe, why should any earthly ruler or celebrity intimidate us?

When God sends us into the marketplace as His ambassadors, the key to success is not our intelligence, education, or other human qualifications. It is whether we accurately reflect the One who sent us, as Jesus reflected the character of His Father. (See John 14:9.) Yes, an ambassador's character is of the utmost importance. And often, a person's true character isn't revealed until he faces times of pressure and crisis. When the heat is on, we see whether someone is motivated by *self* or by *service*.

L – Leader

The goal of every disciple in training should be to grow as an ambassador and then as a leader. The ultimate gold medal in God's kingdom is to be a leader who not only runs the race but who also finishes well.

One of the keys to successful leadership is to know God's purpose and calling for your life. God does not want you imitating someone else; He wants you to be who He has called you to be. Ultimately, every leader is called to equip other leaders (see Ephesians 4:11–12), but a leader will never succeed in that unless he has first discovered his own spiritual DNA and destiny. Every leader is called to be a change agent, but he must first discover which of the seven realms of culture his primary assignment is in.

Once you've received clarity on your calling as a leader, you will be tested. Nehemiah is a great book on leadership, illustrating seven ways every one of us will be tested by our enemies:

1. Ridicule and mockery (See Nehemiah 4:1.)

2. Threats of attack by enemies (See Nehemiah 4:14–23.)

3. Discouragement (See Nehemiah 4:10.)

4. Division (See Nehemiah 5:1.)

5. Compromise (See Nehemiah 6:1–2.)

6. Slander (See Nehemiah 6:5–7.)

7. Fear (See Nehemiah 6:13–14.)

Sometimes, a young believer may view Christian leadership as glamorous, but it's anything but that. The higher our position, the more we will have to die to ourselves, putting the interests of others above our own. Like Nehemiah, we will face criticism and scorn; and like Jesus our Master, we will inevitably suffer persecution, rejection, and even betrayal.

While mentoring his spiritual son Timothy, Paul made it very clear that he was inviting him to a battlefield, not a bed of roses. Rather than offering Timothy the perks many leaders expect today—such as a lucrative salary, health insurance, and a retirement plan—Paul simply said,

You therefore must endure hardship as a good soldier of Jesus Christ. No one engaged in warfare entangles himself with the affairs of this life, that he may please him who enlisted him as a soldier.

(2 Timothy 2:3–4)

And later he added,

All who desire to live godly in Christ Jesus will suffer persecution.
(2 Timothy 3:12)

So do you still want to be a leader? If so, get ready for some hardships and battles. In order to successfully reach the finish line and be one of God's gold medalists, you'll have to be tenacious, resilient, and persevering. But I have good news! As the chorus of the old hymn says so well,

It will be worth it all when we see Jesus;
Life's trials will seem so small when we see Christ;
One glimpse of His dear face all sorrow will erase;
So bravely run the race till we see Christ.[25]

So let us press on to run the race. Our Lord is ready to strengthen and encourage us today, and He will be awaiting us at the finish line.

---

25. Esther Kerr Rusthoi, "When We See Christ," 1941.

24

Why Your Revival Tarries

In 1959, Leonard Ravenhill wrote a classic book called *Why Revival Tarries*. In it, he described some reasons why the church doesn't see revival:

> We're content to live without it. It's too costly. We don't want God to disrupt our status quo. The Christian life can only be lived one way, and that's God's way. And God's way is that I leave all and follow Him.... When I think I've "arrived" at something, the Lord shutters that.[26]

Ouch. I sure hope I never become content to live without revival. I never want to conclude that a spiritual awakening is too costly, or that the status quo is preferable to a move of God's Spirit throughout our nation. But I know that each of us must guard against spiritual complacency. If Christians in the early church lost their first Love and became lukewarm, how much more do we have to take pains to ensure that our own hearts remain kindled with fresh passion for God?

One of the things I love about the book of Hebrews is its recurring theme of believers standing strong in the Lord and finishing their journey of faith well. The writer also lists at least ten specific hindrances to personal and corporate revival. Nearly every believer claims to desire a transformed

---

26. Ravenhill, *Why Revival Tarries*.

life, but these ten factors often get in the way. Today, as in the day Hebrews was written, every Christian will face the following hindrances:

1. Failure to hate sin (See Hebrews 1:9; 12:1; 13:18.)

2. Negligence (See Hebrews 2:1–3.)

3. Hardening of heart (See Hebrews 3:7–15.)

4. Unbelief (See Hebrews 3:12, 19; 10:38–39; 11:6.)

5. Prayerlessness (See Hebrews 4:16; 5:7–8.)

6. Dullness of hearing (See Hebrews 5:11–14.)

7. Insulting the Spirit of grace (See Hebrews 10:26–29.)

8. Discouragement (See Hebrews 6:11–12, 19–20; 10:23, 35–36; 12:12–13.)

9. Harboring unforgiveness and bitterness (See Hebrews 12:14–15.)

10. Refusing the Lord when He speaks (See Hebrews 12:25–27.)

Taking a Closer Look

I hope you will take time to study this list and review the Scriptures. But now, let's take a closer look at each of these ten hindrances you will face as you seek to fulfill God's destiny for your life.

Failure to Hate Sin

The famous movie actress Mae West said many years ago, "I generally avoid temptation unless I can't resist it." I'm afraid many professing Christians have a very similar philosophy today. They love to quote verses about God's forgiveness when they fall (see, for example, 1 John 1:9), but they don't truly hate the things God hates.

In stark contrast to this cavalier attitude toward sin, we read that Jesus...

...loved righteousness and hated lawlessness; therefore God, [His] God, has anointed [Him] with the oil of gladness more than [His] companions. (Hebrews 1:9; see also Psalm 45:7)

Is this your testimony too, my friend? Can you honestly say that you love righteousness and hate lawlessness? This verse contains a beautiful promise. When we truly set our hearts on loving the things God loves and hating the things He hates, we will experience a new outbreak of joy in our lives. While the world says that a person serious about the things of God will become just an old religious fuddy-duddy, the truth of the matter is just the opposite. The Lord will anoint that person with an extraordinary dose of *"the oil of gladness."*

So the writer of Hebrews encourages us to *"lay aside every weight, and the sin which so easily ensnares us"* (Hebrews 12:1). Why? So we can *"run with endurance the race that is set before us"* (verse 1). This is not a matter of trying to impress people by our godliness, for the Lord is our Judge in this race we're running. In everything we do, our objective should be to maintain a *"good conscience"* (Hebrews 13:18) before the Lord.

Negligence

Is there something very precious in your life that you've taken for granted? Perhaps it's an important relationship with your spouse or your children. Or maybe God has blessed you with a nice house or car, but you've neglected to maintain them as well as you should. The writer of Hebrews warns us not to be lulled asleep or take our salvation for granted.

We must give the more earnest heed to the things we have heard, lest we drift away. For if the word spoken through angels proved steadfast, and every transgression and disobedience received a just reward, how shall we escape if we neglect so great a salvation...? (Hebrews 2:1–3)

These should be very sobering words for us. Could we be so negligent that we *"drift away"* from the Lord? Could we be so foolish as to *"neglect so great a salvation"*? Have you taken your relationship with the Lord for granted? Do you need to return to the foundational spiritual disciplines to grow in intimacy with Him? Before I go any further, I encourage you to pause and pray for God to search your heart on this issue.

Hardening of Heart

The Israelites in the wilderness were a primary example of a people who hardened their hearts to God's voice and His ways. Sometimes it's easy to forget that every action, attitude, and decision in the Christian life is ultimately a matter of the heart. Jesus said that the Pharisees did an impressive job of honoring God with their pious words but that their hearts were far from Him. (See Matthew 15:8.) And then He warned, *"Out of the heart proceed evil thoughts, murders, adulteries, fornications, thefts, false witness, blasphemies"* (Matthew 15:19).

So if the heart is so important in our life and our leadership, how do we keep our hearts tender before the Lord? Proverbs 4:23 tells us to guard our heart at all costs:

Keep your heart with all diligence, for out of it spring the issues of life.
(Proverbs 4:23)

Guard your heart above all else, for it determines the course of your life.
(Proverbs 4:23 NLT)

Keep vigilant watch over your heart; that's where life starts.
(Proverbs 4:23 MSG)

One Sabbath day, Jesus was teaching in a synagogue and encountered a man with a withered hand. The religious leaders thought it was scandalous to heal someone on the Sabbath, and they were intent on finding reasons to accuse the Lord if He did. Before Jesus healed the man, we're told that He looked around at the religious leaders and was *"grieved by the hardness of their hearts"* (Mark 3:5).

Notice the vivid contrast between the Lord's tender heart for those bound by sickness, sin, and spiritual oppression, and the proud, calloused hearts of the Jewish leaders. Jesus' compassion for the least and lost must be ours if we are truly His followers.

Unbelief

Scripture says that it is *"impossible"*—not merely difficult—to please God without exercising faith. (See Hebrews 11:6.) The writer of Hebrews also says that unbelief is one of the primary reasons the Israelites were unable to enter the Promised Land. (See Hebrews 3:19.)

This is such an important issue that Paul warned, *"Whatever is not from faith is sin"* (Romans 14:23). In other words, every word we speak or action we take, if not motivated by faith, is actually sin! And this includes even actions that are considered religious or spiritual. Unless we are operating in faith, we're just engaging in dead works.

Prayerlessness

Leaders who are on their knees are not likely to fall. In contrast, leaders who are on pedestals are in great danger of falling off. Which are you on?

It's stunning that Jesus' disciples never asked Him how to preach, heal the sick, or cast out demons; instead, they said, *"Lord, teach us to pray"* (Luke 11:1). As they watched the life and ministry of Jesus, they instinctively recognized that prayer was the secret of His power. Everything else, including His preaching, healing, and deliverance ministry, flowed from His devotion to spending regular time alone with the Father.

If Jesus, the Son of God, needed to pray, how much more do we need to pray? He set a wonderful pattern for us follow: *"Now in the morning, having risen a long while before daylight, He went out and departed to a solitary place; and there He prayed"* (Mark 1:35). He sacrificed His time,

PROVOKE-A-THOUGHT:

"WE NEED PRAYERS OF DESPERATION AND HEARTFELT PASSION, RATHER THAN PRAYERS OF FORMULA AND PLATITUDES, IF WE ARE GOING TO SEE TRANSFORMING REVIVAL."

rising *"long before daylight."* He then found *"a solitary place"* where He could pray without distractions. Each of us must develop a disciplined pattern of prayer, as well.

Dullness of Hearing

One of the greatest promises Jesus gave us is this: *"My sheep hear My voice, and I know them, and they follow Me"* (John 10:27). When dullness of hearing sets in, we must take prompt action to find out what the problem is. Every Christian—especially every Christian leader—must make this a top priority.

Think of it this way: If you're listening to the radio or watching TV and the reception starts getting fuzzy, you probably won't immediately call the radio or TV station to complain. No, first you will try to reset your TV or cable system, checking if there is a problem on the receiving end, because you know there's rarely a problem with the transmitter.

The same principle applies to hearing from the Lord. He loves to speak to His children, and He speaks loud and clear 24/7. So if we aren't hearing anything, we probably need to wax out our ears. We need to deal ruthlessly with anything that is hindering us from clearly hearing His voice.

King David discovered that God was not impressed with his *"sacrifice and offering"* (Psalm 40:6). Rather, David said that the key to becoming a person after God's heart was opening his ears to the Lord and delighting in His will. (See Psalm 40:6, 8.)

Insulting the Spirit of Grace

One of the most serious and most important debates in the church today concerns the nature of God's grace in our lives. Some Bible teachers treat grace as a blank check, enabling them to sin all they want, because they can always ask for forgiveness later. This perspective totally misses the point, as the author of Hebrews describes quite graphically:

If we sin willfully after we have received the knowledge of the truth, there no longer remains a sacrifice for sins, but a certain fearful expectation of judgment, and fiery indignation which will devour the adver-

saries. Anyone who has rejected Moses' law dies without mercy on the testimony of two or three witnesses. Of how much worse punishment, do you suppose, will he be thought worthy who has trampled the Son of God underfoot, counted the blood of the covenant by which he was sanctified a common thing, and insulted the Spirit of grace?

(Hebrews 10:26–29)

If we *"sin willfully,"* we insult *"the Spirit of grace."* Even worse, it's as if we've *"trampled the Son of God underfoot"* and *"counted the blood of the covenant…a common thing."*

You might ask, What about the Lord's grace and forgiveness? The apostle Paul answered this quite differently than some teachers of grace today:

The grace of God has appeared, bringing salvation to all men, instructing us to deny ungodliness and worldly desires and to live sensibly, righteously and godly in the present age, looking for the blessed hope and the appearing of the glory of our great God and Savior, Christ Jesus, who gave Himself for us to redeem us from every lawless deed, and to purify for Himself a people for His own possession, zealous for good deeds.

(Titus 2:11–14 NASB)

Do you see how this contradicts some of today's hyper-grace teachings? Instead of providing us with a license to sin, God's grace actually empowers us *"to deny ungodliness and worldly desires."* Grace is not meant to cover our sins but to transform our lives. (See 1 Corinthians 15:10.) It's a key part of God's great plan *"to purify for Himself a people for His own possession, zealous for good deeds"* (Titus 2:14).

So why does revival tarry? One of the reasons is a tragic misunderstanding of God's grace.

Discouragement

Jerry Falwell once wrote, "I have never known God to use a discouraged person." The book of Hebrews repeatedly addresses this important issue, telling us how to receive encouragement from the Lord and also exhorting us to encourage one another.

The truth of the matter is this: Every one of us has been discouraged at one time or another, and those of us who are leaders are even more prone to bouts of frustration and discouragement when dreams are denied or delayed. But when our heart is downcast and our head is hanging amid life's storms, we need to remember these words:

> *Strengthen the hands which hang down, and the feeble knees, and make straight paths for your feet, so that what is lame may not be dislocated, but rather be healed.* (Hebrews 12:12–13)

Discouragement can knock the wind out of you and act like a powerful and depressing drug. Proverbs 13:12 says, *"Hope deferred makes the heart sick,"* so we need to maintain our vision of hope and destination, fixing our eyes on Jesus. (See Hebrews 12:1–2.)

Don't give up, my friend! Don't throw away your faith or your confidence in the Lord. (See Hebrews 10:35.) Open your heart to encouragement from your fellow leaders and, even more important, learn to encourage yourself in God's presence. (See 1 Samuel 30:6.)

In my own life, I've seen a strong connection between discouragement and a loss of hope. That's why it's so important to fix our hope on God's faithfulness rather than on our circumstances or abilities. (See Hebrews 10:23.) Our hope needs to be anchored to God's unchanging promises in the unseen realm, *"the Presence behind the veil"* (Hebrews 6:19).

Harboring Unforgiveness and Bitterness

As a leader, you are bound to face rejection, misunderstanding, and injustice. Sorry to break it to you, but these things just go with the territory. So the question is whether you will be able to forgive and release the people who wrong you. Will you take the high road? Or will you allow unforgiveness and bitterness to take root in your heart?

Hebrews 12:14–15 warns about allowing a *"root of bitterness"* to take root, which will *"cause trouble"* and defile many other people. When a leader gives place to a bitter, unforgiving spirit, it can affect his entire organization or congregation. Enmity breaks out, division is created, and God's blessings are hindered—all because of unforgiveness.

Refusing the Lord When He Speaks

From time to time, the Lord reminds each of us that He is God and we are not. Every time He speaks to us, we have a decision to make. Will we submit and comply? Or will we resist and rebel? Scripture says that in order to align our lives with God's unshakeable kingdom, we must hear and obey His voice. (See Hebrews 12:25–29.)

No matter what sphere of society we're called to impact, this principle is crucial. Once I was in a pastors' meeting with South Korean pastor David Yonggi Cho, who pastored the largest church in the world at that time. There was a question and answer time, and someone asked him how he had founded such a huge church. "First you pray. Then you obey," Cho explained.

Cho's success strategy sounds pretty simple, doesn't it? This principle applies to every sphere of influence, whether you are in ministry, business, education, or entertainment. Make sure you take time to pray, listen, and obey.

Are You Ready for Revival?

Before we move on, I encourage you to review these ten hindrances to revival. Do some of them apply to your life today? Is your leadership awakening being thwarted by these deterrents?

In my leadership seminars, I often share the story of how at least six other ships warned the *Titanic* about icebergs in its path. But the captain refused to heed the warnings. When the Titanic was launched, one of its crew members had arrogantly said, "Not even God Himself could sink this ship," and that complacent attitude ended up costing over 1,500 lives.

Let us humble ourselves and heed God's warnings. Who knows? Perhaps a revival will be sparked this very day as we repent and the Holy Spirit brings us restoration and renewal.

25

A Final Word

Like so many other sports fans I was amazed as I witnessed the incredible championship comeback victory by the Cleveland Cavaliers during the 2016 NBA Finals. The stories and testimonies of both the Golden State Warriors and the Cleveland Cavaliers are quite inspiring. I must admit though, I've always loved underdog comeback stories. My good friend Jim Buchan forwarded me a blog post he wrote about the series entitled, "Victory to Those Who Finish Well." Here is an excerpt from his blog:

> The Cleveland Cavaliers became the winners of the NBA championship. It was quite a success story, especially since the team was down three games to one in a seven-game series before winning three straight games from the Golden State Warriors. The Warriors had been the winningest team in NBA history in the regular season, winning an incredible seventy-three games and losing only nine. But victory, in sports or in life, is seldom a matter of getting off to a good start. Rather, it comes to those who *finish well*. The clutch shots in the final minutes often make all the difference. All the accomplishments or failures of the past tend to be eclipsed by how the game of life ends. I've found that people tend to forget the opening moments but remember the game's finale. The Bible has a lot to say about finishing well. Here's the good news: Even if we see the clock clicking down, there's still time to achieve victory and greater impact before the final buzzer sounds.

The Reviresco Factor

I first heard of the word *reviresco* at a luncheon to recognize volunteerism in Texas. I had been appointed by the Texas governor to serve on the board of a foundation that was hosting the luncheon. As the speaker explained *reviresco* and its meaning, the Lord began to show me some biblical parallels and I became intrigued. I did additional research on the word and discovered that it had been used in some military settings to encourage the troops. At times of discouragement and possible defeat, commanders would declare *reviresco*, signifying that they would rise again and prevail.

Deriving from a Latin word, *reviresco* is an encouragement for us to be overcomers and finish well. According to the *JM Latin English Dictionary*, *reviresco* means "to grow green again; grow strong or young again." This is akin to our English word *revival*, and it reflects biblical promises such as Psalm 103:5, in which God says He'll satisfy you in such a way that "*your youth is renewed like the eagle's.*"

The McEwen clan of Scotland adopted *reviresco* as part of their family motto at a clan revival in the early nineteenth century. Its symbol is a sprouting branch growing out of an oak stump. It signifies and declares that they were destined to overcome and return victorious. I remember talking with a friend, former congressman Bob McEwen, about his family crest and sure enough, *Reviresco* is written on their shield and coat of arms. He graciously sent me a picture of it.

As Christian leaders, God wants us to know that no matter what we may be going through right now, we are "*more than conquerors through Him who loved us*" (Roman 8:37).

We, too, can boldly proclaim, *"Reviresco!"* And like the Cleveland Cavaliers, we, too, shall rise again, overcome, and be victorious. Regardless of our circumstances or hardships, we know that in Christ, we shall be victorious. I've personally experienced the fact that through every adversity, God will show Himself even greater. Second Corinthians 2:14 is a reminder that God will always lead us to triumph so that we can be dispensers of the knowledge and fragrance of heaven to others. Some of the circumstances we encounter in the world around us may have an unpleasant odor, but we are called to manifest the presence of the Lord and to dispense His fragrance everywhere we go and in every situation.

> *Now thanks be to God who always leads us in triumph in Christ, and through us diffuses the fragrance of His knowledge in every place.*
> (2 Corinthians 2:14)

Reviresco is a reminder that no matter what you may be going through today, God can bring you victory and renewal. The Lord can strengthen you with perseverance and courage to rise up and be the leader He has called you to be.

A Call to Finish the Race Well

Paul's letters are peppered with exhortations to his friends and spiritual sons to finish the race well. He told Timothy to *"fight the good fight, keeping faith and a good conscience, which some have rejected and suffered shipwreck in regard to their faith"* (1 Timothy 1:18–19 NASB). This was an

PROVOKE-A-THOUGHT:

"ANYONE CAN START A RACE, BUT DO THEY FINISH IT? SOME RUN HARD AND FAST IN LIFE, BUT DO NOT FINISH WELL. MAY WE LIVE IN SUCH A WAY THAT WE FINISH WELL. THE LIVES WE LIVE BEFORE ENTERING THE PORTALS OF ETERNITY DETERMINES THE LEGACY WE LEAVE."

acknowledgement that Christian leadership is no cakewalk; it's a battle. Timothy would have to hold firmly to God's promises, and he would have to maintain a *"good conscience"* with how he lived his life.

In his letter to the Colossians, Paul sent a message to another young leader: *"Say to Archippus, 'Take heed to the ministry which you have received in the Lord, that you may fulfill it'"* (Colossians 4:17 NASB). What if you or I inserted our own name into this word of encouragement: "Say to Doug [or your name], 'Take heed to the ministry you have received in the Lord, that you may fulfill it.'"

You see, that is the Lord's will for each of us. Not just to start the race, not just to get off to a good start in our career, ministry, or relationships, no, He wants us to finish what we've begun, and to finish well. Paul was confident that he was doing this. I love how *The Message* paraphrases some of his final words to Timothy.

> *You take over. I'm about to die, my life an offering on God's altar. This is the only race worth running. I've run hard right to the finish, believed all the way. All that's left now is the shouting—God's applause!*
> (2 Timothy 4:6–8 MSG)

What a beautiful ending to Paul's story. He had run the race well, and now he was passing the baton to Timothy and a new generation of leaders. He saw the finish line ahead, and instead of just coasting, he ran with all his might.

Paul knew he had something incredible to look forward to: *"God's applause!"* That is my objective today, and I hope it is yours as well. We may not always receive accolades and applause, but that's okay. The applause of heaven is what really matters.

Someone is waiting for you and me at the finish line. We'll be able to recognize Him by the nail-pierced scars on His hands and feet.

PROVOKE-A-THOUGHT:

"SOME RUN HARD AND FAST IN LIFE, BUT DO NOT FINISH WELL. ANYONE CAN START A RACE, BUT NOT ALL FINISH. RUN WELL; FINISH WELL."

He has already completed His race, and He's cheering us on to finish ours. If we run well, we will hear the most awesome greeting any man or woman could ever hear. Our heavenly Father will say,

> *Well done, good and faithful servant; you were faithful over a few things, I will make you ruler over many things. Enter into the joy of your lord.*   (Matthew 25:21)

Until that day, my friends, "*Reviresco!*"

About the Author

D r. J. Doug Stringer is founder and president of Turning Point Ministries International and Somebody Cares America/International (SCA/SCI), which was recognized in the May/June 2014 issue of *Ministry Today* magazine as one of the twenty-one churches or ministries that are most influencing the twenty-first-century church. Doug's years of ministry have taken him to numerous communities and nations—from urban to foreign missions, from garbage dumps to the palaces and halls of government leaders. As an Asian-American, Doug is considered a bridge-builder of reconciliation amongst various ethnic and religious groups.

Somebody Cares has implemented several citywide strategies now multiplied in cities across the nation. Over the years, Somebody Cares has become a model for connecting needs with resources during natural calamities, including the Japan earthquake/tsunami, the Texas wildfires, the Haitian earthquake, the Indian Ocean tsunami, and Hurricanes Katrina, Rita, and Ike. Through the expansion of the disaster preparedness and relief collaborations, the ministry has established the Global Compassion Response Network.

Doug has served on several disaster relief panels, including a forum hosted by the Heritage Foundation, based in Washington, DC. Doug served on the OneStar Foundation by appointment by the governor of Texas. He also serves on the international advisory board of the Geneva Institute for Leadership and Public Policy. He serves on various local, national, and international boards, including the Christian Men's Network and the Global Fatherhood Initiative. He serves as co-chair for the Billion Souls Initiative and for Mission America's Love2020 Initiative, as well as on the advisory boards of ministries such as Youth-Reach Houston, Coreluv for Orphans, Seniority Services, Inc., and others.

Doug is the author of *In Search of a Father's Blessing, It's Time to Cross the Jordan, The Fatherless Generation, Somebody Cares, Born to Die, Hope for the Fatherless Generation,* and *Living Life Well.*

Doug resides in the greater Houston, Texas, area with his wife, Lisa, and daughter, Ashley.

For more information, visit www.dougstringer.com.